low carb
fresh & flavorful

low carb
fresh & flavorful

Amanda Cross

hamlyn

First published in Great Britain in 2004 by
Hamlyn, a division of
Octopus Publishing Group Ltd
2–4 Heron Quays, London E14 4JP

ISBN 0 600 61098 5

A CIP catalog record for this book is available
from the British Library

Printed and bound in China

10 9 8 7 6 5 4 3 2 1

NOTES

Both metric and imperial measurements are given for the recipes. Use one set of measures only, not a mixture of both.

Ovens should be preheated to the specified temperature. If using a convection or forced-air oven, follow the manufacturer's instructions for adjusting the time and temperature. Broilers should also be preheated.

This book includes dishes made with nuts and nut derivatives. It is advisable for those with known allergic reactions to nuts and nut derivatives and those who may be potentially vulnerable to these allergies, such as pregnant and nursing mothers, invalids, the elderly, babies, and children, to avoid dishes made with nuts and nut oils. It is also prudent to check the labels of preprepared ingredients for the possible inclusion of nut derivatives.

Meat and poultry should be cooked thoroughly. To test if poultry is cooked, pierce the flesh through the thickest part with a skewer or fork—the juices should run clear, never pink or red.

All the recipes in this book have been analyzed by a professional nutritionist. The analysis refers to each serving.

Low Carb Fresh & Flavorful is meant to be used as a general reference and recipe book to aid weight loss. However, you are urged to consult a health-care professional to check whether it is a suitable weight-loss plan for you, before embarking on it.

While all reasonable care has been taken during the preparation of this edition, neither the publishers, editors, nor the author can accept responsibility for any consequences arising from the use of this information.

Contents

Introduction

Following a low-carbohydrate diet is the latest celebrity craze but because many people have taken it to unhealthy extremes, low-carb eating has received some bad press and caused huge controversy the world over.

Nonetheless, common sense alone suggests that we should all be looking at reducing our intake of complex carbohydrates and eliminating unhealthy refined carbohydrates, which are playing a major contributory role in a worldwide obesity epidemic and the upsurge of degenerative diseases.

Refined carbs may be very convenient and have a long shelf life, but they do little for our health. And for people who are overweight, in particular, eating such foods will only exacerbate the problem.

If refined carbs form a regular or staple part of your diet, it may be beneficial to think again about what you eat. Eating a diet heavy in refined foods can be disastrous for your health as it can lead to obesity and a number of serious diseases, including cancers, bowel and heart problems, and diabetes. The only people who benefit from poor diets are:

- **dentists**—who deal with your decaying teeth
- **pharmaceutical companies**—who sell you the drugs to deal with your ailing immune systems and chronic, degenerative diseases
- **food manufacturers**—who are only really interested in profit

So, far from being a fad, it is vital for your future health that you avoid the refined carbohydrates in favor of a modest amount of unrefined carbohydrates, as well as all the alternatives that are provided in this book.

Refined carbs are damaging your health

Even though complex carbohydrates are a vital component of our overall food intake, refined carbohydrates serve no nutritional purpose whatsoever. When food is mass-produced and processed, it is stripped of fiber and nutrients.

For example, when flour and sugar are turned from brown to white in order to make them look more appealing, they become nutritionally redundant. Processing flour and sugar removes magnesium, zinc, and chromium, the three minerals the body needs to metabolize carbohydrates effectively. It also drastically reduces the presence of vitamins B_1, B_2, B_3, calcium, and iron.

Junk foods are mostly made up of refined flour and sugar, as well as processed fats, colorings, flavorings, and preservatives, which are equally devoid of nutrients. Worryingly, these foods make up 75 percent of many people's diets.

Refined carbs and obesity

In 1995, the World Health Organization (WHO) released figures estimating that 200 million adults worldwide were obese. By 2000, the figures had increased to 300 million. Unfortunately the problem is not just restricted to adults—25 percent of children and adolescents in the US are also overweight. The problem is now so great that it is beginning to replace malnutrition and infectious diseases as the most significant contributor to ill health in the world. In fact, obesity is now recognized as a disease in its own right, and one that is largely preventable through changes in lifestyle, especially diet.

Risks associated with obesity

Being overweight can lead to:

- **Diabetes (type 2: noninsulin dependent)**
- **Coronary heart disease and stroke**

It also increases the risks of:

- **Cancer of the colon, prostate, uterus, cervix, breasts, and ovaries**
- **Gallbladder disease**
- **Musculoskeletal disorders and respiratory problems**

Recent studies have shown that "overweight" and "obese" are terms that could be applied to more than half the adult population throughout the world. Surprisingly, this is true not only for the Western world but many developing countries too. The cause of this accelerating problem of obesity is a sedentary lifestyle coupled with a high intake of refined carbohydrates.

Does your diet include large amounts of these foods?

- White bread and bread products
- White rice
- Refined sugar
- Salt
- Carbonated drinks
- Bottled cordials and "juice" drinks (like orangeade or lemonade)
- Candies
- Chocolate
- Margarine
- Cookies and cakes
- Potato chips and salted nuts
- Canned fruit and vegetables
- Processed meat products such as hamburgers and sausages
- Sugary cereals
- Sweetened low-fat fruit yogurts
- Ice cream and popsicles
- White pasta
- Prepackaged convenience meals
- Sauces and gravy mixes
- Take-out foods such as pizza and Chinese food

Refined carbs and blood glucose imbalance

Convenience foods are full of empty calories that deplete the body's supply of the essential vitamins and minerals it needs to perform important functions. They are stripped of their natural fiber, which is essential for the body to be able to control insulin production and protect against diseases such as diverticulitis and colon cancer. When eaten in excess, refined carbohydrates crash into the bloodstream and cause damage to insulin and blood glucose levels, creating severe imbalances.

Many people who eat a diet high in the wrong sorts of carbohydrate suffer from a condition called "Syndrome X" or insulin resistance, which in simple terms means their bloodstream becomes flooded with excess glucose. This in turn triggers excess insulin production, to the point where the body ceases to become responsive to this blood-balancing hormone. This results in less glucose being converted into energy and more being laid down as fat.

One of the roles of insulin is to send messages of hunger to the brain, so excess insulin simply results in more and more cravings for carbohydrate-laden food. The symptoms of unstable blood glucose are listed to the left.

If you are suffering from more than one of these symptoms then it may be worth reviewing your diet, because maybe your health isn't as good as it should be. Additionally, and more importantly, you could be creating more serious problems for your health in the future.

How carbohydrates work in the body

Refined carbohydrates should be avoided entirely if possible and replaced with the far more healthy complex carbohydrates, such as vegetables and brown rice. These are a vital part of the human diet and are our primary source of energy. In their natural state they can be turned by the body into glucose to provide fuel for the different organs of the body.

However, even the more natural sources of carbohydrates can have a negative effect on energy levels, as they all vary in the rate at which they are absorbed into the bloodstream. Individual energy requirements also correlate to the amount of energy expenditure, so a person who doesn't get enough exercise and eats a diet too high in carbohydrates will often have problems with their weight.

If you want to control your carbohydrate intake, you will need to understand more about how carbohydrates work and also about how they are classified. Carbohydrates can be categorized in three ways: by type, by Glycemic Index (GI), and by density value.

The most basic carbohydrate of them all is glucose. This has the "simplest" structure and is assimilated immediately by the body. The more complex the structure of the sugar, the longer it takes the body to convert it into energy—thus "complex" carbohydrates are the slow-burners in carbohydrate terms, as they are higher in more complicated sugars and fiber, and so generally take longer to break down into energy-giving glucose.

Types of carbohydrate

- **Simple sugars or monosaccharides: glucose (blood sugar), and fructose (fruit sugar)**

- **Double sugars or disaccharides: lactose (milk sugar)**

- **Complex carbohydrates or polysaccharides: starches and cellulose (potatoes, rice, grains and dietary fiber)**

Glycemic Index (GI)

Carbohydrates have a glycemic value that indicates how quickly they can be metabolized by the body and converted into glucose. The ones with the highest GI are those that will have the most profound and immediate effect on your blood glucose levels—cooked potatoes and white rice are both at the upper end of the scale.

The higher the GI value of a food, the more likely it is to induce surges in blood glucose levels. So high-GI foods are to be avoided in favor of low-GI foods.

Carefree Carbohydrates
Low-GI foods

Eat freely from this list.

Arugula, asparagus, bean sprouts, beet greens, beets, bell peppers, broccoli, Brussels sprouts, cabbage, cauliflower, celeriac, celery, chives, collard greens, cucumber, dandelion leaves, eggplant, endive, kale, kohlrabi, leeks, lettuce, mustard greens, okra, onions, parsley, pimento, pumpkin, radishes, rutabaga, spinach, string beans, Swiss chard, turnips, watercress.

Apples, apricots (fresh), blackberries, blueberries, cantaloupe, cranberries, grapefruit, guava, kiwis, lemons, limes, loganberries, oranges, papayas, peaches, plums, raspberries, rhubarb, strawberries, tangerines, tomatoes, watermelon.

Careful Carbohydrates
Medium-GI foods

Eat moderately from this list. These foods can send your carb levels soaring if eaten to excess. The more active you are, the more you can afford to include these foods in your diet.

Artichokes, bananas, brown rice, carrots, cherries, corn, dried beans (legumes), dried fruit (any), figs, grapes, honey, kumquats, lentils, lima beans, mangoes, mulberries, parsnips, peas, pears, pineapple, pomegranates, potato, prunes, rye bread, squash, sweet potato, yam.

Careless Carbohydrates
High-GI foods

Avoid eating foods from this list. You can exist without any of them, so have them only occasionally.

Processed food with high flour and sugar content, such as cookies, pastries, and cakes, white bread and bread products, white rice, refined sugar, carbonated drinks, bottled cordials and juice "ade" drinks, candies, chocolate, sugary cereals, sweetened low-fat fruit yogurt, ice cream, and frozen popsicles, white pasta, prepackaged convenience meals, sauces and gravy mixes, take-out foods such as pizzas, curries, and Chinese food.

Density value of Carbohydrates

Carbohydrates are also evaluated on their density value. This is the amount of usable carbohydrate in relation to fiber and water content. The more fiber and water a vegetable or fruit contains, the fewer usable carbohydrates it will have. The densest carbohydrates are legumes, whole grains, and starchy vegetables—which also feature highly on the Glycemic Index—the least dense are leafy green vegetables, especially when eaten raw.

DENSITY VALUES OF COMMON CARBOHYDRATES

Less than 1 g carb*

4 oz (125 g) alfalfa sprouts 0.4 g

1½ oz (40 g) arugula 0.4 g

3 oz (75 g) bok choy 0.8 g

1 stalk celery 0.9 g

1½ oz (40 g) endive 0.8 g

3 oz (75 g) lettuce 0.4 g

1½ oz (40 g) radicchio 0.9 g

5 radishes 0.8 g

Less than 3 g carb*

6 fresh asparagus spears 2.4 g

2 oz (50 g) raw beet tops 1.8 g

2 oz (50 g) blackberries 2.9 g

6 oz (175 g) raw broccoli 2.2 g

6 oz (175 g) cauliflower florets 2.6 g

½ medium cucumber 3 g

1½ oz (40 g) leeks 2 g

1½ oz (40g) raw mushrooms 1.1 g

3⅓ oz (90 g) cooked mushrooms 2.3 g

2½ oz (75 g) raw onion 2.5 g

1½ oz (40 g) parsley 1.9 g

3⅓ oz (90 g) red bell pepper 2.4 g

Less than 5 g carb*

½ medium avocado 3.7 g

3 oz (75 g) green beans 3.8 g

1 oz (25 g) blueberries 4.3 g

4 Brussels sprouts 3.4 g

7 oz (200 g) red or green cabbage 3.6 g

1 whole chili pepper 4.3 g

1½ oz (40 g) chopped dandelion
   leaves 3.3 g

4 oz (125 g) eggplant 4 g

2 oz (50 g) fresh fennel 3.1 g

3 oz (75 g) mustard greens 4 g

3½ oz (100 g) strawberries 3.3 g

1½ oz (40 g) Swiss chard 3.6 g

1 medium tomato 4.3 g

3 oz (75 g) canned water chestnuts
   4.5 g

*Per serving

Changing to a healthy, low-carb diet

The recipes in this book have been designed to help you create a healthy low-carb lifestyle. If you are trying to lose weight, aim to restrict yourself to around 2–3⅓ oz (50–90 g) carbohydrates per day and concentrate on eating plenty from the "carefree" list—raw when possible.

For weight management and a more balanced approach to your diet, incorporate small portions of healthy complex carbohydrates such as brown rice, whole-wheat or rye bread, potatoes, or whole grains into your meals.

Eat more raw fruit and vegetables

By increasing your intake of the low-glycemic-value fruit and vegetables in the carefree list, you will be on your way to becoming leaner as well as much healthier. Phyto-nutrients, found in brightly colored, raw, organic fruit and vegetables, can protect you from ill health in many different ways. Sadly, these are deficient in many people's diets. Phyto-nutrients can help regulate the immune system, stabilize vitamins in body tissue, and give protection from serious illnesses such as cancer by acting as antioxidants and fighting free radicals. Although they are not classed as essential nutrients, without them your sense of well-being will be severely compromised. They work in the body at deep physiological and biochemical levels and can be found easily in the low-density and low-glycemic fruit and vegetables included in a low-carb diet.

Cooking destroys many of the phyto-nutrients present in the carefree list of colorful, energy-boosting fruit and vegetables, so eating them raw (whenever possible) is the key to getting the maximum benefit from their life-enhancing properties.

A healthy diet is about getting the right balance between the three macro-nutrients: proteins, carbohydrates, and fats. But, more importantly, the *type* of protein, carbohydrate, and fat you eat is key, so it is important to remember that eating protein and fat with carbohydrate slows down the rate at which the glucose in the carbohydrate hits the bloodstream, thereby helping to balance your energy levels.

Eat high-quality protein

Our body is comprised mainly of protein, which, after water, is the most abundant substance in the body and is the major constituent of muscle, tissue, skin, hormones, enzymes, antibodies, and blood. Continuing on after childhood, protein plays a vital role in maintaining and rebuilding our bodies as they cope with the wear and tear of daily life.

It is better for you to eat organic meat and fish whenever possible. Meat from an animal that is allowed to roam and graze on grass is high in omega-3 fatty acids and is of a superior quality to the meat from grain-fed animals, which tends to be high in carbohydrates and omega-6 fatty acids. Non-organic meat is also often from animals who have been pumped full of antibiotics and growth hormones. Likewise, fish that are caught in the wild are far less fatty than their counterparts that have been farmed in restrictive conditions. Although it is not always possible to buy free-range, organic meat and fish, do try to buy the best that you can afford.

Eat the right fats

You need fats in your diet. Your brain consists mostly of fat, and your intelligence, heartbeat, and muscular movements all depend on that fat cushioned inside your head. The only way your body can send electrical messages through living tissue is through your nerve cells and their connectors—and these are made out of fat. Therefore some fats, also known as lipids, are essential.

Fat types

There are two main types of natural fats: saturated and unsaturated:

- **Saturated fats** come primarily from animal sources such as meat and dairy produce, as well as from coconut and palm kernel oil, and are solid at room temperature. Their main job is to provide the body with a stored form of energy in the fat cells.

- **Unsaturated fats** are found in vegetables, nuts, grains, and seeds, and also in fish and game. These are liquid at room temperature.

Results of fat deficiency

- Muscle weakness
- Impaired vision
- PMS
- Emotional and behavioral problems
- Raised cholesterol levels
- Poor immunity
- Premature aging
- Heart disease
- Arthritis-like symptoms
- Male sterility
- Nervous disorders
- Depression
- Dry skin and eczema

Good protein choices

- **Meat** Organic beef, pork, lamb, bacon, and ham

- **Poultry and Game** Organic or free-range chicken, pheasant, quail, turkey, wild duck, rabbit, venison, and wild boar

- **Fish and Shellfish** Cod, mackerel, sardines, trout, tuna (fresh)—all rich in omega-3 fatty acids; bass, clams, crab, crayfish, flounder, haddock, halibut, herring, lobster, green-lipped mussels, oysters, porgy, scallops, shrimp, snapper, squid, swordfish, tuna (canned).

- **Eggs**

- **Cheese—maximum 3¾ oz (110 g) as a portion occasionally—** Parmesan, Camembert, feta, cottage, ricotta

- **Vegetarian options** Tofu, tempeh, and other soy products with a low-carb content

- **Microfiltered whey protein powder**

Poor protein choices

- Fatty bacon, sausages, salami, processed meat products, fish fingers, fish fried in batter, fish cakes, crabsticks, chicken nuggets.

Good fat sources

- Almonds
- Avocado
- Coconut oil
- Fish: oily fish, such as salmon, tuna, and herring
- Flax-seed oil and flax seeds
- Hemp oil and hemp seeds
- Leafy vegetables
- Macadamia nuts
- Olive oil
- Olives
- Peanut butter
- Pumpkin seeds
- Sunflower seeds
- Tahini
- Tofu
- Walnuts
- Whole grains

Unsaturated fats contain two fatty acids that are essential to life. More importantly, these are fats that the body cannot produce itself. They are linoleic acid (omega 6) and linolenic acid (omega 3) and your body can make all the other fatty acids it needs.

Saturated fats get a lot of bad press and a diet too heavy in saturated fats has been closely linked to cardiovascular disease. But there is another fat that has the capacity to do as much (if not more) harm than an excessive intake of saturated fats and that is a chemically altered hydrogenated fat such as margarine. This type of fat can interfere with the metabolism of some essential fatty acids. Research has shown that the trans fats in hydrogenated fats can increase the LDL (bad) cholesterol, decrease the HDL (good) cholesterol, and thus increase the risk of coronary heart disease.

Hydrogenated fats exist in almost all processed foods in the supermarket, as well as in frozen convenience foods and deep-fried fast food. This is another good reason to stop eating junk food and try to eat as much fresh, natural produce as possible.

Fiber and water

No healthy diet would be complete without water and fiber. If you eat plenty of raw vegetables you will be eating plenty of fiber, and make sure you drink a minimum of 6–8 glasses of water per day to keep you hydrated.

Unsaturated fats

Saturated fats

Hydrogenated fats

Just add exercise

Exercise is vital. You could eat the healthiest diet in the world, take nutritional supplements, and avoid alcohol and cigarettes, but still not be physically fit. Overall health is incomplete without physical activity. In the words of the super-slim veteran of svelte, Joan Collins: "If you don't use it—lose it." You need to do two types of exercise to be fit and look lean.

- **Aerobic exercise**

  This includes cycling, running, swimming, and walking—in fact any exercise that raises your heartbeat and makes you take in more oxygen. Aim to do 30–45 minutes of aerobic exercise three or more times each week.

- **Resistance or weight training**

  To exercise your muscles you can use free weights, weight machines, or rubber bands, or do pushes, lunges, or other gravity-resistant exercises including workouts in water. This type of exercise increases your energy levels, burns fat, and strengthens joints and bones. There are also many other benefits: for example, your metabolism will increase for many hours after a good workout (one 60-minute workout will result in 24 hours of raised metabolism) and you will experience increases in rejuvenating growth hormone levels.

  The real benefit is that, as you lose fat and start to build more muscle, you will actually burn calories more effectively. The correct exercise will help rid you of your tendency to gain weight, among a whole host of other benefits, if you do it regularly.

Calorie-burning activities

Even the most mundane tasks can burn off calories, so next time you are faced with a mountain of ironing, be happy in the knowledge that you are burning off 252 calories an hour.

Activity	Calories (Kcals) used per hour
Bedmaking	234
Bowling	264
Cleaning windows	350
Cycling (5½ mph (9 km/h))	210
Dancing	330
Desk work	132
Soccer	450
Gardening	250
General housework	190
Golfing	300
Horseback riding	480
Ironing	252
Jogging	500
Mowing the lawn	462
Running	900
Skiing	594
Swimming	500
Walking (2½ mph (4 km/ph))	116

Caution

Before you start any exercise regime, check your overall fitness with your doctor or a qualified gym instructor.

- Builds muscle and increases strength
- Burns more calories
- Reduces body fat
- Lowers insulin levels
- Helps to ward off illness and degenerative disease by boosting immunity
- Increases bone density
- Increases glucagon
- Reduces blood pressure and triglyceride levels
- Increases HDL—good cholesterol
- Lowers blood pressure
- Reduces the risk of cardiovascular disease, type-2 diabetes, and premature aging
- Alleviates stress and depression by altering brain chemistry
- Boosts overall energy and aerobic fitness

Health benefits

- Boost your metabolism
- Increase the supply of oxygen to your muscles for burning fat
- Increase your Lean Body Mass (LBM) to fat ratio in favor of muscle

Putting it all together

Now you can put your new knowledge to work by making a commitment to change your diet, do more exercise, and develop a new attitude to food and eating. You'll find that, as you start to eat differently, you'll be able to lose excess fat and stabilize your weight at a level that is comfortable for you to maintain.

Low carb, not no carb

It is important to remember that a low-carb diet is not a no-carb diet. But it does mean cutting out "junk" food and focusing instead on healthy ingredients that will fuel your body and mind. With a low-carb diet, you can expect to:

- Lower your insulin levels and stabilize your blood glucose levels.
- Banish food cravings.
- Eliminate energy peaks and troughs and mood swings.
- Enhance your concentration.
- Reeducate yourself into a way of eating that will increase your vitality and improve your overall health.
- Help your body to burn fat and normalize your weight.

Who should follow a low-carb diet?

It may be that you are genetically disposed to gain weight when exposed to an unhealthy diet and lifestyle, or have developed insulin resistance as a result of a diet based on high levels of unhealthy, refined carbohydrates and complex carbohydrates. If this is the case, then a low-carb diet that restricts the amount and type of carbohydrate foods you eat may be the right choice for you.

If you are suffering from any ongoing health problems, take regular medication, are under 20 or over 65 years old, or have any specific nutritional needs, then it is recommended that you check your health status with your doctor before starting a new exercise or eating regime.

The recipe for success

- **Be adaptable**

  All menus can be adapted—swap salmon for tuna, turkey for chicken, or beef for lamb. If you are out of spinach, try a little arugula, use walnut oil instead of olive oil in a dressing, or replace the balsamic vinegar with lemon juice. If you are out of crème fraîche and have only plain strained yogurt, it doesn't matter! Experiment—that is the joy of cooking.

- **Moderation and common sense**

  Nobody is able to watch what they eat 24 hours a day, but it is important to learn the art of moderation. Aim for 85 percent of your diet to be exemplary and allow yourself to eat what you like for the remaining 15 percent. Use your common sense. If given the choice of a spoonful of white sugar or a spoonful of honey—choose the honey—at least it is a natural, complete product that hasn't been stripped of vital nutrients. It is better to have a baked potato than mashed potato, as the skin in the potato has lots of good fiber, essential for slowing down digestion and moderating your insulin.

- **Don't make excuses**

  Many people use their busy lifestyles as an excuse for relying on convenience foods. None of the recipes in this book take more than 30 minutes to prepare, and several are designed to be prepared the day before and cooked in less time than it takes to throw a salad together. So, make the effort—your body will thank you for it.

- **Low carb isn't no carb!**

  The recipes in this book are varied, nutritional, and above all, delicious. Whether you enjoy them as part of a low-carb regime or simply because you prefer a lighter way of eating, this book can help you to find the balance that suits you.

Carbs provided by 3½ oz (100 g) of each of the following foods

Brown bread	44 g
Rye bread	45 g
Broccoli, cooked	1.8 g
Cooked carrots	5 g
Peas, cooked	10 g
Baked potato	31 g
New potatoes boiled in skins	15 g
Brown rice, cooked	32 g
White rice, cooked	30 g
Green salad	1.8 g
Whole-wheat spaghetti, cooked	23 g
Tomato, raw	2.8 g

Asparagus and Prosciutto Wraps

This is a lovely way to serve three simple ingredients, cured ham, asparagus, and mozzarella, to make the perfect light snack or appetizer. If you can't get hold of prosciutto or Parma ham, use Serrano ham or back bacon instead.

Serves 3
Preparation time 10 minutes
Cooking time 28 minutes

1 Trim the asparagus spears and plunge them into a large saucepan of boiling salted water. Cook over a medium heat for 4–8 minutes, or until tender but still crunchy.

2 Drain and plunge into cold water. When they have cooled, drain once again and set aside.

3 Preheat the oven to 400°F.

4 Cut the mozzarella into 18 equal slices. Separate the prosciutto into 6 even piles and cut the butter into 12 even-sized pats.

5 Take 3 asparagus spears and place them on 1 slice of prosciutto. Put 2 pieces of mozzarella in between the spears, along with a small pat of butter. Wrap the prosciutto around the asparagus, using all the slices in the pile.

6 Repeat until you have 6 bundles.

7 Lightly grease an oven dish with some butter and arrange the asparagus bundles over the base. Place a slice of mozzarella and a pat of butter on each bundle. Season with the pepper and bake at the top of the oven for about 20 minutes.

18 thick, fresh asparagus spears

8 oz (250 g) mozzarella

8 oz (250 g) prosciutto, sliced thinly

⅓ cup plus 1 tablespoon (75 g) butter (plus a little extra for greasing)

pepper

Nutritional values per serving
Carbs 2.5 g
Fat 26 g
Protein 43 g
Kcals 415

Shrimp à la Plancha

This makes a tasty snack or first course. Buy the best shrimp you can find. If using frozen shrimp, be sure to defrost them thoroughly in the fridge overnight.

Serves 4
Preparation time 2 minutes
Cooking time 7–10 minutes

1 Heat the oil in a shallow flameproof casserole dish or a skillet with a lid, add the garlic and chili, and season with salt and pepper. Fry until the garlic begins to brown.

2 Arrange the shrimp in the base of the casserole dish or skillet and baste with the flavored oil. Cover and cook for about 5 minutes, or until the shrimp have turned pink.

3 Serve scattered with parsley or cilantro and the lemon wedges on the side.

½ cup (125 ml) olive oil

8 garlic cloves, chopped

½–1 dried red chili, seeded and crushed

16 raw jumbo shrimp

salt and pepper

To serve

2 tablespoons chopped fresh parsley or cilantro

lemon wedges

Nutritional values per serving

Carbs 3.5 g

Fat 30 g

Protein 12.5 g

Kcals 350

Onion Frittata

Almost anything can be put into a frittata or Spanish omelette. This version is great as a lunch dish and can be served with a mixed salad. For a variation, try adding your favorite herbs or spices, Parma ham, shrimp—whatever takes your fancy.

Serves 4
Preparation time 5 minutes
Cooking time 20 minutes

1 lb (500 g) red onions, very finely sliced

6 tablespoons olive oil

6 eggs

½ cup (50 g) freshly grated Parmesan

2 heaping tablespoons (40 g) butter

salt and pepper

1 Put the onions and the olive oil in a large skillet. Heat gently and cook the onion over a very low heat until they soften and caramelize, turning a rich golden brown.

2 Move all the onions to one side of the skillet, then tilt the skillet so the oil drains away from them. Remove the onions with a slotted spoon and keep to one side.

3 Beat the eggs together in a large bowl, then add the onions and the Parmesan. Season with salt and pepper and stir thoroughly to combine all the ingredients.

4 In a medium skillet, about 12 inches (30 cm) in diameter, melt the butter over a medium heat. As soon as it begins to foam, pour the egg mixture into the skillet. Turn the heat down very low.

5 After about 15 minutes, when the eggs have set and thickened and only the surface is runny, place the skillet under a medium broiler for about 1 minute or until the surface of the frittata has set.

6 Loosen the frittata and slide onto a plate, allow to cool slightly, and cut into wedges.

Nutritional values per serving

Carbs 9 g

Fat 35 g

Protein 7.5 g

Kcals 380

Gazpacho

This light, vitamin-packed soup is ideal for a summer detox and for boosting the immune system. Fennel is a natural diuretic and also rich in phyto-estrogens, making it good for calming hot flashes. The soup will only take 30 minutes to make, but it is best served very cold, so allow time to chill it overnight in the refrigerator.

Serves 4
Preparation time 5 minutes
Cooking time 25 minutes, plus chilling time

1 Put the tomatoes in a large pan or bowl and pour over enough boiling water to cover, then leave for about 1 minute. Drain, skin the tomatoes carefully, and then roughly chop the flesh.

2 Trim the green fronds from the fennel and discard. Finely slice the bulb and put it in a saucepan with 1¼ cups (300 ml) salted boiling water. Cover and simmer for 10 minutes.

3 Meanwhile, crush the coriander seeds and peppercorns in a mortar and pestle, heat the olive oil in a large saucepan, and add the crushed spices, garlic, and onion. Cook gently for 5 minutes.

4 Add the vinegar, lemon juice, tomatoes, and oregano, putting a few leaves of the oregano aside for the garnish. Give the mixture a good stir and then add the fennel along with the cooking fluid, tomato paste, and rock salt. Bring to a simmer and leave to cook uncovered for 10 minutes.

5 Whiz in a food processor or blender. Cool and chill overnight, or for at least several hours. Serve garnished with the oregano leaves and the green olives, finely sliced.

1½ lb (750 g) ripe tomatoes

1 large fennel bulb

¾ teaspoon coriander seeds

½ teaspoon mixed peppercorns

1 tablespoon extra-virgin olive oil

1 large garlic clove, crushed

1 small onion, chopped

1 tablespoon balsamic vinegar

1 tablespoon lemon juice

¾ teaspoon chopped oregano

1 teaspoon tomato paste

1 rounded teaspoon kosher salt

green olives and oregano leaves, to garnish

Nutritional values per serving
Carbs 10 g
Fat 4.5 g
Protein 2.5 g
Kcals 88

Spinach, Lentil, and Lemon Soup

This tangy soup is the perfect energy-boosting light lunch or appetizer. Lentils are a great source of B vitamins and an excellent way of providing protein for vegetarians.

Serves 4
Preparation time 5 minutes
Cooking time 25–30 minutes

1 Heat the oil in a large saucepan over a medium heat, add the leeks and garlic, and cook for 6 minutes, or until golden.

2 Add the bay leaves, thyme, oregano, stock, and lentils to the pan. Cook for 20 minutes, stirring occasionally.

3 Add the spinach and lemon juice to the soup and cook for a further 2 minutes. Season with salt and pepper and serve.

1 tablespoon olive oil

3 leeks, finely chopped

4 garlic cloves, crushed

3 bay leaves

4 thyme sprigs

4 oregano sprigs

5 cups (1.2 liters) vegetable stock

2¼ cups (425 g) canned green or Puy lentils, drained

1 lb (500 g) fresh spinach, trimmed and chopped

⅓ cup (75 ml) lemon juice

salt and pepper

Nutritional values per serving

Carbs 26 g

Fat 6.5 g

Protein 16.6 g

Kcals 225

Onion and Fennel Soup

This is a quick and easy variation on the classic French onion soup.
The herbs and fennel give it a fresh twist. If you haven't got any fennel,
then celery will work just as well. Serve piping hot on a winter's day.

Serves 4
Preparation time 5 minutes
Cooking time 20–25 minutes

1 tablespoon olive oil

6 medium onions, chopped

2 tablespoons chopped thyme

1 tablespoon rosemary leaves

5 cups (1.2 liters) vegetable or beef stock

2½ cups (600 ml) water

14 oz (425 g) fennel, finely sliced

salt and pepper

Parmesan shavings, to garnish

1 Place the oil in a large saucepan and warm gently over a low heat.

2 Add the onions, thyme, and rosemary to the saucepan and cook for 10 minutes.

3 Add the stock, water, and fennel to the saucepan and cook, uncovered, over a medium heat for 10–15 minutes. Season to taste with salt.

4 Ladle the soup into serving bowls and garnish with Parmesan shavings and black pepper.

Nutritional values per serving

Carbs 19 g

Fat 7.7 g

Protein 8.5 g

Kcals 160

Chicken Satay

With so many people on high-protein diets, this is likely to be a popular dish at cocktail parties as it is so low in carbohydrates. Even better, any of your guests who are not following a diet will enjoy it too. It's useful to have a few easy-to-make recipes like this up your sleeve.

Serves 12
Preparation time 10 minutes
Cooking time 10 minutes, plus marinating time

1 In a large mixing bowl, combine the peanut butter, soy sauce, lime juice, curry powder, garlic, and hot pepper sauce.

2 Place the chicken in the marinade and leave to marinate for about 12 hours or overnight in the refrigerator.

3 When ready to cook, preheat the broiler to high. Put the chicken onto skewers and broil for 5 minutes on each side.

4 Serve immediately.

2 tablespoons (25 g) smooth peanut butter

½ cup (125 ml) soy sauce

½ cup (125 ml) lime juice

2 heaping tablespoons (15 g) curry powder

2 garlic cloves, chopped

1 teaspoon hot pepper sauce

6 skinless chicken breast halves, cubed

Nutritional values per serving

Carbs 1.5 g

Fat 2.7 g

Protein 21 g

Kcals 115

Shiitake Mushroom Omelette

Even the most basic of dishes can be given a more exotic twist with a little imagination. If you can't get hold of shiitake mushrooms, then crimini mushrooms, finely sliced, will work just as well. Miso paste is a Japanese fermented soybean paste. It has the consistency of peanut butter and comes in a wide variety of flavors and colors. Many large supermarkets stock it, as do Asian food stores.

Serves 2
Preparation time 5 minutes
Cooking time 5 minutes

1 Heat the oil in a skillet over a medium heat. Add the mushrooms and chives, and stir-fry for 2 minutes.

2 Dissolve the miso in the boiling water and add to the skillet. Continue to fry until the liquid has evaporated.

3 Pour the eggs over the mushroom mixture and swirl around the pan to form a thin omelette. Cook for 1 minute.

4 Remove the pan from the heat and slide the omelette onto a plate. Roll up and sprinkle with pepper and a few extra chives.

2 teaspoons sesame oil

1½ cups (125 g) shiitake mushrooms, sliced

3 tablespoons chopped chives, plus extra to garnish

1 teaspoon miso paste

¼ cup (50 ml) boiling water

5 eggs, lightly beaten

pepper

Nutritional values per serving
Carbs 1.3 g
Fat 20 g
Protein 18 g
Kcals 270

Jerusalem Artichoke Hummus

A lighter version of conventional hummus, this is excellent served with vegetable crudités as a snack or appetizer. It could also be served as an unusual sauce for barbecued chicken.

Serves 6
Preparation time 10 minutes
Cooking time 5 minutes

12 oz (375 g) Jerusalem artichokes, scrubbed

¼ cup (50 g) butter

⅔ cup (150 ml) chicken stock

1 cup (250 g) canned chickpeas, drained

1 teaspoon ground cumin

2 tablespoons lemon juice

1 garlic clove, crushed

1 Place the artichokes in a saucepan of boiling water and cook for 5 minutes or until tender, then drain.

2 Put the cooked artichokes in a blender or food processor with the butter and stock, and process until smooth.

3 Add the chickpeas, cumin, lemon juice, and garlic. Process again until smooth. Serve with crudités or whole-wheat pita bread.

Nutritional values per serving

Carbs 12 g

Fat 1.15 g

Protein 3.7 g

Kcals 69

Fresh Fava Bean and Herb Dip

This delicious dip originates from Egypt, though I have substituted fresh or frozen beans for the usual dried ones, which gives it a bright green color and a wonderful fresh taste. Fava beans are also a good low-carb choice as they contain less carbohydrate per ounce than, for example, Great Northern beans.

Serves 4
Preparation time 5 minutes
Cooking time 15 minutes, plus chilling time

1 Put the beans into a saucepan of boiling salted water and boil for 5 minutes.

2 Add the herbs, cover, and simmer for a further 5 minutes. Strain and reserve some of the cooking liquid.

3 Combine the beans with the chilies, garlic, cumin, 2 tablespoons of the oil, and 3–4 tablespoons of the reserved cooking liquid in a food processor.

4 Process to a smooth paste, season to taste, and add a little more cooking liquid if it is too dry. Put into a serving dish and chill.

5 Put the rest of the oil in a nonstick skillet and fry the onion briskly until golden and crisp. Spread over the dip and serve with crudités or whole-wheat pita bread.

2⅓ cups (375 g) fresh or frozen fava beans

1 cup (50 g) parsley, coarsely chopped

3 cups (50 g) cilantro, coarsely chopped

1–2 fresh green chilies, seeded and chopped

2 garlic cloves, chopped

1½ teaspoons ground cumin

3 tablespoons olive oil

1 onion, thinly sliced

salt

Nutritional values per serving

Carbs 12 g

Fat 12 g

Protein 8 g

Kcals 190

Asian Tuna Salad

This salad is incredibly simple to make and very healthy. Tuna is full of omega-3 fatty acids, so it is brain-boosting into the bargain. You can replace the fresh tuna with canned if it's more convenient, but you should then omit the marinating and cooking stage, and simply add the wasabi paste and sake to the dressing.

Wasabi is a Japanese horseradish sauce. It has a pungent, fiery, and sharp flavor and comes as a paste and a powder. Sake is Japanese rice wine, although some consider it to be a beer because it is made from a grain. Whatever the distinction, dry white wine is a good substitute.

Serves 4
Preparation time 15 minutes
Cooking time 1 minute, plus marinating time

1 Combine the tuna with the soy sauce, wasabi, and sake. Set aside to marinate for 10 minutes.

2 Arrange the salad greens, tomatoes, and cucumber on serving plates.

3 Make the dressing by combining all the ingredients in a bowl or screw-top jar.

4 Heat a nonstick skillet over a high heat and fry the tuna for about 10 seconds on each side, or until seared. Place the tuna on top of the salad, drizzle with the dressing, and serve.

12 oz (350 g) tuna steak cut into bite-sized chunks

3 tablespoons soy sauce

1 teaspoon wasabi paste

1 tablespoon sake or dry white wine

8 cups (200 g) mixed salad greens

1 cup (150 g) baby yellow tomatoes, halved

1 cucumber, sliced into thin wide strips

For the dressing

2 tablespoons soy sauce

1 tablespoon lime juice

1 teaspoon brown sugar

2 teaspoons sesame oil

Nutritional values per serving

Carbs 6.5 g

Fat 7 g

Protein 22.5 g

Kcals 178

Radicchio, Artichoke, and Walnut Salad

This salad is the perfect accompaniment to a simple grilled or broiled steak—but its earthy flavors also make it a great meal in its own right.

Serves 4
Preparation time 10 minutes
Cooking time 15 minutes

1 Peel the artichokes and cut them into bite-sized chunks. Bring a saucepan of water to a boil. Add half the lemon juice and the artichokes to the saucepan and boil for 5–7 minutes. Drain thoroughly.

2 Meanwhile, separate the radicchio leaves and arrange them in a large flameproof dish. Scatter the walnuts over the leaves, sprinkle over the oil, and season. Cook under a medium broiler for 2–3 minutes. Remove from the broiler.

3 Turn the broiler to high. Add the cooked, drained artichokes to the radicchio salad, then sprinkle with the remaining lemon juice and zest and season with salt and pepper.

4 Broil the salad until the artichokes begin to brown. Serve scattered with the parsley.

1 lb (500 g) Jerusalem artichokes

zest and juice of 1 unwaxed lemon

1 head radicchio weighing about 5 oz (150 g)

⅓ cup (40 g) walnut pieces

3 tablespoons walnut oil

salt and pepper

flat-leaf parsley, to garnish

Nutritional values per serving
Carbs 14 g
Fat 18 g
Protein 3.7 g
Kcals 226

Romaine Lettuce Salad with Gorgonzola and Walnuts

This satisfying salad makes a good appetizer or light lunch. Any blue cheese will work equally well, and any crisp green lettuce can be substituted for the Romaine. If you really want to rev up the walnut flavor, use half walnut oil and half olive oil.

Serves 4–6
Preparation time 10 minutes

5 tablespoons olive oil

1 tablespoon good white wine vinegar

½ teaspoon salt

4 oz (125 g) Gorgonzola

½ cup (50 g) shelled walnuts, coarsely chopped

1 Romaine lettuce, torn into bite-sized pieces

pepper

1 Put the oil, vinegar, salt, and a little black pepper into the salad bowl and mix thoroughly. Add half the Gorgonzola and mash it well with a fork.

2 Add half the chopped walnuts and all the lettuce, and toss until evenly coated with the dressing. Season to taste.

3 Top with the remaining Gorgonzola, cut into small pieces, and the rest of the chopped walnuts.

Nutritional values per serving

Carbs 0.7 g

Fat 24 g

Protein 5 g

Kcals 250

Warm Puy Lentil and Goat Cheese Salad

A great winter salad with North African flavors, combine this with a bowl of soup for a filling lunch or light supper. Halloumi cheese works well instead of goat cheese, especially with a little drizzle of chili oil.

Serves 4
Preparation time 10 minutes
Cooking time 20–30 minutes

1 Heat the oil in a saucepan over a medium heat. Add the cumin seeds, garlic, and ginger, and cook for 1 minute.

2 Add the lentils and cook for a further minute.

3 Pour the stock into the saucepan one ladleful at a time, waiting until the liquid has been absorbed before adding more (about 20–30 minutes). Remove the pan from the heat and stir in the mint and cilantro with a squeeze of lime.

4 To serve, place the spinach leaves in individual bowls, top with a quarter of the lentils and the goat cheese, and sprinkle with black pepper.

2 teaspoons olive oil

2 teaspoons cumin seeds

2 garlic cloves, crushed

2 teaspoons grated fresh ginger root

⅔ cup (125 g) Puy lentils

3¼ cups (750 ml) chicken or vegetable stock

2 tablespoons chopped mint

2 tablespoons chopped cilantro

½ lime

5 cups (150 g) baby spinach leaves

4 oz (125 g) goat cheese

pepper

Nutritional values per serving

Carbs 18 g

Fat 13 g

Protein 12 g

Kcals 250

Eggplant and Chickpea Salad

This is a robust salad that will keep even the most ardent meat-eater happy. Eggplants contain calcium, beta-carotene and folic acid and are a natural detox food.

Serves 4
Preparation time 20 minutes
Cooking time 7 minutes

1 Place the eggplant in a colander, sprinkle with salt, and leave to drain for 20 minutes. Rinse and dry on paper towels.
2 Heat the oil in a skillet over a high heat. Add the garlic, coriander, cardamom, and cinnamon, and cook for 1 minute. Add the eggplant and cook, stirring continuously, for 3 minutes, or until golden.
3 Add the chickpeas and cook for a further 3 minutes. Stir in the parsley and remove the skillet from the heat.
4 Make the dressing by combining all the ingredients. To serve, place the spinach on serving plates, top with the eggplant mixture, and drizzle with the dressing.

2 eggplants, chopped into bite-sized chunks

3 tablespoons olive oil

3 garlic cloves, crushed

2 teaspoons ground coriander

1 teaspoon cardamom seeds

1 teaspoon ground cinnamon

¾ cup plus 2 heaping tablespoons (200 g) cooked or canned chickpeas

¼ cup (15 g) flat-leaf parsley, chopped

6½ cups (200 g) baby spinach leaves, washed and drained

salt

For the dressing

½ cup (125 ml) plain yogurt

2 tablespoons chopped mint

2 teaspoons honey

2 teaspoons ground cumin

Nutritional values per serving
Carbs 15 g
Fat 13 g
Protein 7.5 g
Kcals 205

Caprese Salad

A salad that makes a simple appetizer for 6 or a light lunch for 4 if served with a green salad. As with all simple dishes, the key is to use good-quality ingredients, so buy really ripe organic tomatoes and really fresh buffalo mozzarella.

Serves 4–6
Preparation time 10 minutes

1 lb (500 g) beefsteak tomatoes, sliced

2 balls of mozzarella, sliced

3 tablespoons Simple Vinaigrette (see page 123)

2 tablespoons chopped basil

salt and pepper

1 Arrange the tomato and mozzarella in overlapping slices on a serving plate.

2 Drizzle with the vinaigrette.

3 Scatter with fresh basil and season with salt and freshly ground black pepper.

Nutritional values per serving

Carbs 3 g

Fat 14 g

Protein 13 g

Kcals 195

Warm Scallop Salad with a Wild Strawberry Dressing

This gorgeous salad combines a great selection of low-carb ingredients and is the perfect choice for a dinner party appetizer or light lunch. If you can't get hold of wild strawberries, use small organic ones with lots of flavor. You could even allow yourself a little glass of dry champagne to complete the decadence.

Serves 4
Preparation time 10 minutes
Cooking time 2½ minutes

1 Begin by making the dressing. Puree the strawberries, vinegar, lemon juice, and olive oil in a food processor. Pass the sauce through a fine sieve or muslin cloth to remove the seeds and then set aside.

2 Season the scallops with salt, pepper, and lemon juice.

3 Next make the garnish. Heat the oil in a nonstick skillet over a high heat. Add the leeks and fry for 1 minute, or until golden brown. Set aside.

4 In the same skillet, fry the scallop slices for 20–30 seconds on each side. Divide the salad greens into 4 portions and pile in the center of individual serving plates. Arrange the scallop slices over the salad.

5 In a small saucepan, gently heat the strawberry dressing for 20–30 seconds, then pour over the scallops and salad greens.

6 Scatter over the fried leeks and garnish with the wild strawberries. Sprinkle with a little freshly ground black pepper and serve.

1¾ cups (250 g) wild strawberries, hulled

2 tablespoons balsamic vinegar

1 tablespoon lemon juice

¼ cup (50 ml) olive oil

12 king scallops, without corals, cut into 3 slices

juice of 1 lemon

6 cups (250 g) mixed salad greens

salt and pepper

For the garnish

1 tablespoon olive oil

3 leeks, cut into julienne (matchstick-thin) strips

20 wild strawberries or 8 larger strawberries, sliced

Nutritional values per serving
Carbs 12 g
Fat 17 g
Protein 22 g
Kcals 300

Green Olive and Ruby Grapefruit Salad

This dish combines sharp, salty, creamy, and bitter tastes to perfection. Pomegranate molasses is actually a juice with a syrupy consistency. It is both tart and sweet with a satisfying rich aftertaste. The best place to find it is in a Middle Eastern supermarket, as it is particularly popular in Turkish cuisine. If you can't get hold of pomegranate molasses, then try a mixture of lime juice and light corn syrup.

Serves 4
Preparation time 10 minutes, plus standing time

1 Place the olives, grapefruit, watercress, hazelnuts, and avocado on a serving plate.
2 Mix together the molasses, olive oil, salt, and pepper, and pour over the salad.
3 Before serving, allow the salad to stand for 10 minutes so the flavors have a chance to infuse.

2 cups (250 g) green olives, pitted

2 ruby grapefruit, peeled and sliced into segments

2 watercress sprigs

½ cup (50 g) roasted hazelnuts, chopped

1 avocado, chopped

1 tablespoon pomegranate molasses

2 tablespoons olive oil

salt and pepper

Nutritional values per serving

Carbs 6.5 g

Fat 33 g

Protein 5.7 g

Kcals 345

Avocado, Crab, and Cilantro Salad

This is a very satisfying salad and an excellent choice for lunch. If you are feeling extravagant, buy 4 extra crab claws and add them to the finished dish. You could add a few baby new potatoes, too, if you are not too worried about raising the carb level.

Serves 4
Preparation time 10 minutes

1 head frisée

6 cups (175 g) corn salad (or baby spinach leaves)

1 large ripe avocado, sliced

10 oz (300 g) crabmeat

10 oz (300 g) fresh mango, cubed (1 large mango)

1 heaping cup (175 g) cherry tomatoes, halved

a pinch of ground nutmeg

salt and pepper

For the dressing

5 tablespoons olive oil

1 tablespoon lime juice

3 tablespoons chopped fresh cilantro

1 small red chili, seeded and finely chopped (optional)

Nutritional values per serving

Carbs 14 g

Fat 34 g

Protein 17 g

Kcals 430

1 First, make the dressing. Put all the ingredients in a jar and shake until well combined, or whiz them briefly in a blender.

2 Divide the frisée and corn salad (or baby spinach) among 4 serving plates.

3 Scatter the avocado, crabmeat, mango, and tomatoes over each portion.

4 Season with salt, pepper, and nutmeg. Drizzle the dressing over the salads and serve.

Smoked Salmon and Quails' Egg Salad

Try to source organic wild salmon rather than its farmed counterpart. The quality of the fish will be much better—it is not as fatty for a start. Quails' eggs can usually be found in good supermarkets, but if you have difficulty getting hold of them, use 6 free-range hens' eggs instead.

Serves 4
Preparation time 15 minutes
Cooking time 3 minutes

12 quails' eggs

7 oz (200 g) baby asparagus, ends trimmed

1 red leaf lettuce

1 head frisée

8 oz (250 g) smoked salmon

juice of 1 lime

salt and pepper

a few sprigs of fresh chervil, to garnish

For the dressing

zest and juice of 2 unwaxed lemons

½ teaspoon English mustard

1 egg yolk

6 tablespoons olive oil

Nutritional values per serving

Carbs 1.9 g

Fat 6.25 g

Protein 20 g

Kcals 142

1 Boil the eggs for 3 minutes (4–6 minutes for hens' eggs, depending on how you like them), then drain and cool under cold running water. Peel and place the eggs in salted water, then set aside until required.

2 Meanwhile, place the asparagus in a saucepan of boiling water and cook on a medium heat for 3–5 minutes or until tender. Drain and cool under cold running water and set aside.

3 Make the dressing by placing the lemon juice and zest, mustard, and egg yolk in a food processor or blender. Whiz quickly to combine the ingredients thoroughly, then, on a low speed, add the oil in a steady stream. Pass the dressing through a fine sieve and season to taste.

4 Wash the lettuce and frisée, and separate the leaves, removing any tough stalks. Put the leaves in a bowl and add two-thirds of the dressing. Toss to distribute the dressing evenly, then arrange in the center of 4 serving plates.

5 Divide the salmon into 4 portions, then drape over the salad leaves. Sprinkle with a little lime juice. Halve the eggs (quarter the hens' eggs) and arrange them over the salad. Drizzle with the remaining dressing, garnish with the sprigs of chervil and serve.

Duck Breasts with Lentils and Mandarin Marmalade

Duck is often associated with hours of laborious cooking in the oven, but duck breasts are very quick and a great alternative to the ubiquitous chicken.

Serves 4
Preparation time 10 minutes
Cooking time 20 minutes

1 Preheat the oven to 400°F. Place the duck breasts in a shallow roasting pan, skin side up, and roast in the oven for 10–15 minutes. They should still be pink in the middle after this time. Allow them to rest in the pan for 5 minutes after being removed from the oven.

2 Meanwhile, put the lentils into a pan of salted water, bring to a boil, and boil for 15 minutes.

3 While the duck and lentils are cooking, start making the marmalade by placing the orange juice and mandarins in a stainless-steel saucepan. Bring to a boil, then reduce the heat and cook for 10 minutes or until reduced by two-thirds.

4 Start making the sauce at the same time as the marmalade by gently sweating the shallots in a nonstick skillet for about 2–3 minutes. Add the port and grape juice. Boil for about 10 minutes, or until the sauce has reduced by half.

5 When the duck has rested, remove it from the saucepan and set aside. Skim off the excess fat from the saucepan. Add the cooked lentils and chicken stock to the saucepan.

6 Place the pan over a medium heat on the stove and cook rapidly for about 2–3 minutes, scraping the pan to incorporate any meat solids, until the stock has nearly evaporated. Slice the duck breasts.

7 Put one-quarter of the warmed lentils on each plate. Top with the sliced duck breast. Spoon a little mandarin marmalade over the meat. Pour the sauce around the lentils and serve garnished with chervil.

4 duck breasts weighing 6 oz (175 g) each

1 scant cup (175 g) Puy lentils

⅔ cup (150 ml) chicken stock

salt and pepper

chervil sprigs, to garnish

For the marmalade

1¼ cup (300 ml) orange juice

8 oz (250 g) finely chopped mandarin oranges, seeded but with peel left on

For the sauce

3 shallots, finely chopped

¼ cup (50 ml) port

⅔ cup (150 ml) red grape juice

Nutritional values per serving

Carbs 38 g

Fat 73 g

Protein 30 g

Kcals 930

Duck Breasts with Baked Belgian Endive

Fresh plums and tart apples make a refreshing sauce to accompany the duck, perfectly balancing the bitterness of the Belgian endive.

Serves 4
Preparation time 5 minutes
Cooking time 15 minutes

1 Preheat the oven to 425°F.

2 Brush the duck breasts with honey and sprinkle with a little salt. Transfer to a cookie sheet and bake in the oven for 9 minutes.

3 Pour the lemon juice into a saucepan of lightly boiling water and blanch the Belgian endive for 2 minutes. Drain and set aside.

4 Brush the Belgian endive with oil and place alongside the duck. Return to the oven and bake for a further 6 minutes.

5 Meanwhile, make the sauce by putting the apple, plums, stock, and sugar into a saucepan. Bring to a boil and simmer for 10 minutes or until the fruit is very tender. Strain the sauce into a bowl then push the fruit through the strainer, adding the puree to the sauce. Mix and set aside.

6 Stir the sherry and balsamic vinegar into the fruit puree, and season to taste with salt and pepper.

7 To serve, arrange the Belgian endive on a platter, then slice the duck breasts and fan them out on top. Spoon the puree over and accompany with a selection of vegetables.

4 duck breasts weighing 6 oz (175 g) each, scored across the skin

1 tablespoon honey

1 tablespoon lemon juice

4 heads Belgian endive, cut lengthways into quarters

1 tablespoon olive oil

salt and pepper

For the fruit puree

1 cooking apple, peeled, cored, and sliced

3 plums (about 175 g), halved and pitted

⅔ cup (150 ml) vegetable stock

1 teaspoon soft brown sugar

3 tablespoons dry sherry

2 teaspoons balsamic vinegar

Nutritional values per serving
Carbs 14 g
Fat 69 g
Protein 24 g
Kcals 780

Grilled Chicken Breasts with Walnut and Celeriac Cakes

This sounds fiddly but is really quick to make. Celeriac is very low in carbohydrates and the nuts are full of essential fatty acids.

Serves 4
Preparation time 10 minutes
Cooking time 30 minutes

1 large head celeriac, weighing about 14 oz (400 g), peeled

1 garlic clove, finely chopped

1 small onion, finely chopped

2 strips of bacon, cut into short strips

4 teaspoons walnuts, crushed

1 oz (25 g) Cheddar, grated

1 egg white

1 tablespoon olive oil

4 corn-fed chicken breasts, weighing 5 oz (150 g) each

salt and pepper

For the sauce

1¼ cups (300 ml) apple juice

⅔ cup (150 ml) chicken stock

1 cooking apple, grated

Nutritional values per serving

Carbs 23 g

Fat 12 g

Protein 27 g

Kcals 312

1 Cut 4 thin, round slices from the celeriac and grate the rest. Combine the grated celeriac with the garlic, onion, bacon, and walnuts in a nonstick skillet. Cover and sweat for 4 minutes, or until soft.

2 Add the grated cheese and egg white to the skillet and stir to mix thoroughly. Season with salt and pepper. Divide the mixture into 4 portions and, when cool enough to handle, shape into 4 cakes.

3 Place the cakes on a nonstick baking pan and bake in a preheated oven at 425°F for 15 minutes or until golden.

4 Meanwhile, brush the celeriac slices with the oil and place on a broiler rack. Season the chicken breasts and place each one, skin side down, on a celeriac slice. Broil under a medium heat for 4 minutes, then turn and cook a further 5–6 minutes, or until cooked through.

5 Next make the sauce. Pour the apple juice and stock into a saucepan and boil rapidly until reduced by two-thirds. Add the grated apple and remove from the heat.

6 To serve, place a celeriac cake on a warmed plate and top with a chicken breast.

7 Use paper towels to remove any excess fat from the celeriac slices. Pour a little sauce around the chicken and garnish with the celeriac slice. Serve immediately.

Pan-fried Chicken Thighs with Fresh Pesto

This quick, economical dish is great served with fresh vegetables or a spinach salad. If you want to make it even easier, just buy a jar of high-quality pesto instead. A couple of tablespoons per portion will do the job perfectly.

Serves 4
Preparation time 5 minutes
Cooking time 25 minutes

1 First, cook the chicken. Heat the oil in a nonstick skillet over a medium heat. Add the chicken thighs and cook gently, turning frequently until the chicken is cooked through (about 20 minutes).

2 Meanwhile, make the pesto by placing all the ingredients in a blender or food processor and whizzing until smooth and well combined.

3 Remove the chicken from the skillet and keep hot. Reduce the heat and add the pesto to the skillet. Heat through for 2–3 minutes.

4 Pour the warmed pesto over the chicken thighs and serve with steamed vegetables.

1 tablespoon olive oil

8 chicken thighs

basil, to garnish

For the pesto

6 tablespoons olive oil

¼ cup (50 g) pine nuts, toasted

½ cup (50 g) freshly grated Parmesan

1 heaping cup (50 g) basil leaves

¼ cup (15 g) parsley

2 garlic cloves, chopped

salt and pepper

Nutritional values per serving

Carbs 2.5 g

Fat 38 g

Protein 17.5 g

Kcals 425

Chicken Stir-fry with Lemon Grass

This recipe is great because you can make the marinade in advance and leave the chicken overnight in the refrigerator. Cooking the next day will take as long as you need to boil the rice. Or, for a really low-carb meal, serve the chicken with a selection of steamed vegetables.

Serves 4
Preparation time 10 minutes
Cooking time 20 minutes, plus marinating time

1 Place the chicken in a nonmetallic bowl, then add all the marinade ingredients. Mix thoroughly, cover, and refrigerate for 1–24 hours.

2 To cook the chicken, heat the oil in a large wok or lidded skillet over a high heat. When the oil is hot, add the chopped garlic and fry for about 30 seconds, or until golden.

3 Add the chicken and all the marinade, then stir-fry for 5–6 minutes, or until the chicken has browned a little. Add the fish sauce and half the stock. Stir and cover. Cook over a high heat for 5 minutes. Remove the lid and stir, then add the remaining stock and turn the heat to low. Cover and cook for a further 5 minutes.

4 Add the onions and turn the heat back up to high. Fry for 1–2 minutes, stirring continuously.

5 Serve with rice or steamed vegetables and garnished with the cilantro, if desired.

2 lb (1 kg) meaty chicken pieces, roughly chopped into 2-inch (5-cm) chunks

3 tablespoons vegetable oil

5 garlic cloves, finely chopped

1 tablespoon fish sauce

8 tablespoons chicken stock

1 medium-sized (100 g) onion, finely sliced

chopped fresh cilantro, to garnish (optional)

For the marinade

1 stick fresh lemon grass, finely chopped

2 garlic cloves, crushed

½-inch (1-cm) cube fresh ginger, finely grated

1½ teaspoons tomato paste

½ teaspoon salt

¼ teaspoon chili powder

¼ teaspoon ground turmeric

Quick&Easy Tip

If you can't get hold of fresh lemon grass, use dried instead. For this recipe, soak 2 tablespoons of dried lemon grass in 4 tablespoons of hot water for 1 hour.

Nutritional values per serving

Carbs 5 g

Fat 16 g

Protein 81 g

Kcals 490

Cold Chicken with Sesame and Chili Sauce

This dish is otherwise known as Bon-bon Chicken and comes from the Szechuan province of China. It makes a fabulous lunch that is especially delicious served with a simple green salad, keeping the carb count low.

Serves 4
Preparation time 15 minutes
Cooking time 5 minutes

1 lb (500 g) chicken breasts, boned and skinned

1 green onion

1 celery stalk, finely chopped

2½ cups (40 g) fresh cilantro, stalks and leaves

salt

For the sauce

1-inch (2.5-cm) cube fresh ginger, finely grated

1 garlic clove, crushed

2 tablespoons sesame paste

1 tablespoon sesame oil

2½ teaspoons chili oil

4 teaspoons Chinese light soy sauce

½ teaspoon ground roasted Szechuan peppercorns

Nutritional values per serving

Carbs 1.5 g

Fat 16 g

Protein 81 g

Kcals 475

1 First, make the sauce by mixing together all the ingredients in a bowl.

2 Cut the chicken pieces lengthways into ½-inch (1-cm) strips and put into a medium skillet. Pour in enough water to cover the meat by ¼ inch (5 mm) and season with a generous pinch of salt. Add the green onion and celery, and bring to a boil over a high heat, then reduce the heat and simmer for about 5 minutes, or until the chicken is cooked through and white all over.

3 Remove the chicken from the skillet with a slotted spoon and rinse under cold water. Reserve the poaching liquid. Pull the chicken into long shreds and set aside.

4 Chop the cilantro stalks very finely and roughly chop the leaves.

5 Add 3 tablespoons of the poaching liquid to the sauce and stir to combine.

6 Mix together the chicken, celery, cilantro stalks, and sauce. Put the chicken in a serving dish and sprinkle over the cilantro leaves. Serve immediately.

Quick&Easy Tip

Szechuan peppercorns are available from Asian food stores but if you have difficulty finding them, use coarsely ground black peppercorns instead. To roast Szechuan peppercorns, dry-fry them in a small pan until they begin to release their aroma.

Chicken with Red Wine and Grapes

This is a hearty combination of red wine, red onions, red pesto, and red grapes. For a lighter, sharper version, use white wine, green pesto, white onions, and white grapes. If you are not too worried about the extra calories and like a creamy sauce, add a little mascarpone cheese toward the end of the cooking time.

Serves 4
Preparation time 3 minutes
Cooking time 28 minutes

1 Heat 2 tablespoons of the oil in a large skillet. Add the chicken breasts and sauté over a medium heat for 5 minutes, turning frequently. Remove with a slotted spoon and drain on paper towels.

2 Add the remaining oil to the skillet and add the onion slices and pesto. Cook for 3 minutes, stirring constantly, until the onion is softened but not browned.

3 Add the red wine and water to the skillet and bring to a boil. Return the chicken breasts to the skillet and season with salt and pepper. Reduce the heat and simmer for 20 minutes, or until the chicken is cooked through.

4 Add the grapes, stir, and serve immediately, garnished with basil leaves.

3 tablespoons olive oil

4 skinned chicken breasts, weighing 5 oz (150 g) each

1 red onion, sliced

2 tablespoons red pesto (as green pesto but with the addition of sun-dried tomatoes)

1¼ cups (300 ml) red wine

1¼ cups (300 ml) water

1⅓ cups (125 g) red grapes, halved and seeded

salt and pepper

fresh basil, to garnish

Nutritional values per serving
Carbs 7.5 g
Fat 18 g
Protein 50 g
Kcals 443

Braised Quail with Olives

The Spanish love quail, considering it very flavorful. But because these tasty game birds are so tiny, you will need 2 per person for a main meal. This dish is perfect served with a small portion of rice—but don't forget to add the extra carbs to your daily allowance.

Serves 4
Preparation time 10 minutes
Cooking time 30 minutes

1 Truss each quail by tucking the wing tips under the body. Cross the legs and place each in a slit made on either side of the cavity.

2 Heat half the oil in a large flameproof casserole dish or lidded skillet, add the quails, and fry until browned all over. Remove from the dish or skillet and keep warm.

3 Add the remaining oil, onion, and garlic. Fry until softened. Add the remaining ingredients, season, and bring to a boil.

4 Place the quails back in the dish or skillet, cover, and simmer gently for 25 minutes or until tender.

5 Remove the bay leaf and thyme, then transfer the quails to a warmed serving dish. Garnish with the thyme sprigs and serve with a green salad or selection of vegetables.

8 quails

4 tablespoons olive oil

1 onion, finely chopped

2 garlic cloves, finely chopped

4 tomatoes, skinned and chopped

⅔ cup (150 ml) dry white wine

2 tablespoons brandy

½ cup (50 g) green olives, pitted and halved

2 tablespoons chopped fresh parsley

1 bay leaf

1 thyme sprig, plus extra to garnish

salt and pepper

Nutritional values per serving
Carbs 7 g
Fat 26 g
Protein 35 g
Kcals 440

Pan-roasted Chicken with Lemon and Rosemary

One of the greatest mistakes people make with chicken is to overcook it. In fact, chicken is best when cooked quickly and seasoned simply. This dish will be ready by the time you have whipped up a quick salad.

Serves 4
Preparation time 5 minutes
Cooking time 30 minutes

4 chicken breasts, with skin, weighing 5 oz (150 g) each

2 tablespoons olive oil

1 tablespoon (15 g) butter

1 sprig fresh rosemary or 1 level teaspoon dried rosemary

3 garlic cloves, roughly sliced

1 cup (250 ml) dry white wine

2 tablespoons lemon juice

5-6 very thin strips of lemon zest

salt and pepper

1 Rinse the chicken under cold water and place skin-side down in a skillet. Dry-fry the chicken over a medium heat until it is evenly browned on all sides.

2 Add the oil, butter, rosemary, garlic, and seasoning, then cook for 2–3 minutes, turning the chicken pieces once.

3 Add the wine, turn up the heat, and let the wine bubble for about 1 minute.

4 Turn the heat down to medium-low and cover. Cook for 15–20 minutes, or until the chicken is cooked through and still juicy.

5 Remove the skillet from the heat and transfer the chicken to a warmed serving dish. Skim the oil off the surface of the liquid, then add the lemon juice and the zest, and cook over a medium heat for 1 minute, stirring gently. Pour this light sauce over the chicken and serve.

Nutritional values per serving

Carbs 2 g

Fat 20 g

Protein 43 g

Kcals 363

Broiled Cornish Hens with a Citrus Glaze

Cornish hens (also called squab) are incredibly easy to cook in the oven or on the barbecue. In this recipe they are simply broiled while the sharp citrus juices bring out the flavor of the meat beautifully. You can use the same recipe for any small birds, such as quails, pigeons, or partridges.

Serves 4
Preparation time 10 minutes
Cooking time 20 minutes

1 Roll the Cornish hen halves with a rolling pin to flatten them slightly. Place the butter in a small bowl, beat in 1 tablespoon of the olive oil, the garlic, thyme, cayenne, seasoning, half the lemon and lime zest, and 1 tablespoon each of the lemon and lime juice.

2 Carefully loosen the skin of each Cornish hen breast and, using a round-bladed knife, evenly spread the citrus mixture between the skin and breast meat.

3 Preheat the broiler to hot/medium and line a broiler rack with foil. In a small bowl mix together the remaining olive oil, lemon juice, lime juice, and honey.

4 Place the Cornish hens, skin-side up, on the broiler rack and brush with the honey and citrus mixture. Broil on one side for 10–12 minutes, basting once or twice with the juices. Turn and broil for a further 7–10 minutes on the other side.

5 The bird is cooked once the thigh juices run clear when pierced with a knife. Serve with grilled tomatoes and a green salad.

2 Cornish hens, weighing 1½ lb (750 g) each, halved

¼ cup (50 g) butter, softened

2 tablespoons olive oil

2 garlic cloves, crushed

½ teaspoon dried thyme

¼ teaspoon cayenne pepper

grated zest and juice of 1 unwaxed lemon

grated zest and juice of 1 unwaxed lime

2 tablespoons honey

salt and pepper

Nutritional values per serving

Carbs 6.7 g

Fat 45 g

Protein 37 g

Kcals 550

Salmon Baked with Broccoli and Morels

Broccoli is an excellent source of both vitamin C and antioxidants. When combined with an oily fish such as salmon, this dish is not only good for weight loss but it will boost your immune system too.

Serves 4
Preparation time 5 minutes
Cooking time 10 minutes

1 Preheat the oven to 450°F.

2 Heat a nonstick ovenproof skillet over a high heat. Lightly season the skillet with salt and pepper, then add the salmon and cook for 30 seconds on each side. Turn the salmon so it is skin-side down and place the skillet in the oven for 8 minutes.

3 Meanwhile, cook the shallots and the sprig of thyme in a nonstick skillet for 2 minutes. Add the white wine and cook over a high heat to reduce the liquor by two-thirds. Stir in the fish stock and reduce by one-quarter.

4 In a separate pan, gently cook the broccoli with the morels and lime juice for 5 minutes. Remove the sauce from the heat and stir in the crème fraîche and butter. Season to taste, then pass through a fine sieve. Stir the chives into the strained sauce.

5 Remove the salmon from the oven and drain on paper towels.

6 To serve, spoon some of the sauce onto each plate, then add a pile of broccoli and a salmon fillet. Arrange the morels around the fish, drizzle with a little extra sauce and sprinkle with ground black pepper.

4 salmon fillets, weighing 5 oz (150 g) each

2 shallots, finely chopped

1 thyme sprig

½ cup (125 ml) dry white wine

⅔ cup (150 ml) fish stock

7 oz (200 g) broccoli raab, washed and cut into florets

10 oz (300 g) fresh morels, wiped

juice of 1 lime

2 teaspoons crème fraîche

2 tablespoons (25 g) butter

1 cup (50 g) chopped chives,

salt and pepper

Nutritional values per serving
Carbs 2.5 g
Fat 25 g
Protein 39 g
Kcals 415

Steamed Fish with Ginger and Coconut Milk

This dish has deliciously contrasting flavors and is superb served with whole lettuce leaves, cucumber slices, and a mixture of mint, basil, and cilantro leaves.

Serves 4
Preparation time 5 minutes
Cooking time 25 minutes

1 Wash the fish and pat it dry. Put the fish onto a heatproof dish or plate that will fit into your steamer or on a rack in a saucepan. Rub the fish with the salt and season with pepper.

2 Place a sieve over a bowl and cover a plate in paper towels. Heat the oil in a skillet over a medium-low heat.

3 When the oil is hot, put in the garlic slivers and fry until golden. Remove them with a slotted spoon and place in the sieve, then transfer onto the paper towel. Repeat with the onion slices.

4 Combine the oyster sauce with 2 tablespoons of the coconut milk and spread the mixture evenly over the fish. Scatter the ginger, green onions, mushrooms, fried garlic, and half the fried onions over the top.

5 Bring some water to a boil in a steamer pan so it reaches about ¾ inch (1.5 cm) below the plate. Place the plate on the rack and cover. Build up steam over a high heat for 2 minutes, then turn down the heat to medium-high and steam the fish for a further 18 minutes, or until it is just done.

6 Carefully lift the plate from the steamer. Transfer some of the sauce around the fish to a small saucepan, add the rest of the coconut milk, and heat gently.

7 Pour over the fish and scatter with the remaining onions and the peanuts.

8 Serve with a selection of vegetables and a small portion of brown rice, or roll pieces of fish in a lettuce leaf with slices of cucumber and sprigs of fresh herbs.

1½ lb (750 g) fish fillets such as salmon, cod, or mullet, skinned

½ teaspoon salt

2 tablespoons vegetable oil

3 garlic cloves, finely sliced

1 medium-sized (100 g) onion, finely sliced

1½ tablespoon oyster sauce

6 tablespoons coconut milk

1-inch (2.5-cm) cube fresh ginger root, peeled and finely sliced into slivers

2 green onions, finely sliced

4 medium mushrooms, finely sliced

4–5 tablespoons roasted peanuts

pepper

Nutritional values per serving
Carbs 7.8 g
Fat 14 g
Protein 35 g
Kcals 302

Fish Poached in Aromatic Tamarind Broth

Simple white fish is fantastic poached in a light broth full of exotic flavors. Add extra vegetables and a few cooked rice noodles for a more substantial dish. Popular in Indian and Middle Eastern cookery, tamarind is known as the Indian date and, with its sour flavor, is used much like lemon and lime juice in Western cooking.

Serves 4
Preparation time 5 minutes
Cooking time 11–14 minutes

3 cups (50 g) fresh cilantro, with roots attached

2 tablespoons (25 g) coarsely chopped onion

1¼-inch (4-cm) cube fresh ginger root; ¾ chopped coarsely, ¼ cut finely into julienne strips (matchsticks)

1 teaspoon shrimp or anchovy paste, or 1 anchovy fillet

3¼ cups (750 ml) chicken stock

1 tablespoon tamarind paste or 2 teaspoons lime juice

1 teaspoon dark brown sugar

¼ teaspoon salt

1 lb (500 g) thick white fish fillets such as cod, haddock, or halibut, cut into 4-inch (10-cm) cubes

1 green onion, finely sliced

1 Cut the roots off the cilantro and chop them coarsely, reserving the rest of the herb for a garnish. Put the cilantro roots into an electric blender along with the chopped onion, chopped ginger, shrimp paste (or equivalent), and about 3 tablespoons of water. Blend until you have a puree.

2 Put the stock into a medium skillet and add the puree, along with the tamarind paste or lime juice, sugar, and salt. Heat to simmering point and simmer for 5 minutes. Taste and adjust the seasoning, if necessary.

3 Place fish in the skillet and poach for 1 minute. Gently turn the fish and cook for another 5–8 minutes, basting frequently. When the fish is cooked through, remove from the skillet and put onto a wide serving dish.

4 Pour over the poaching liquid, scatter with the green onions, the julienned ginger, and the chopped reserved cilantro. Serve with a small portion of boiled rice and a green salad.

Nutritional values per serving

Carbs 4.5 g

Fat 1.5 g

Protein 23 g

Kcals 123

Fish Fest

It is wonderful to serve shellfish on special occasions. In this dish, a selection of shellfish is cooked in an aromatic sauce that hails from the Catalonia region of Spain. Just make sure you have plenty of chilled white wine ready to serve with it.

Serves 4
Preparation time 20 minutes
Cooking time 15 minutes

1 Cut the lobsters in half lengthways. Remove the sac from the head and the intestinal vein, but leave the brown liver and black coral if there is any. Twist off the claws, discarding the smaller ones. Peel the shrimp, leaving the tails intact.

2 Heat the oil in a large lidded skillet. Add the onion and fry until softened. Pour in the brandy, add the garlic, tomatoes, wine, ground almonds, saffron, bay leaf, and seasoning. Cover the skillet and simmer gently for 5 minutes.

3 Add the lobsters, shrimp, mussels, and parsley, and cook for 5 minutes, until the lobsters are heated through, the shrimp turn pink, and the mussels open. Discard any mussels that do not open and crack open the lobster claws.

4 Transfer to a warmed, shallow serving dish and serve with lemon wedges.

2 small cooked lobsters, each weighing 1 lb (500 g)

8 raw jumbo shrimp

3 tablespoons olive oil

1 onion, chopped

2 tablespoons brandy

2 garlic cloves, chopped

4 ripe beefsteak tomatoes, skinned and chopped

1¼ cups (300 ml) dry white wine

⅓ cup (50 g) blanched almonds, ground

a few saffron strands, soaked in 2 tablespoons boiling water

1 bay leaf

24 mussels, cleaned and beards removed

2 tablespoons chopped parsley

salt and pepper

lemon wedges, to serve

Nutritional values per serving

Carbs 10 g

Fat 21 g

Protein 35 g

Kcals 432

Squid with Tomatoes

This Spanish-inspired recipe is not only easy to make but also great served with a salad to make a low-carb dish. It is equally good with rice or pasta if you are serving guests who are not following a low-carb regime.

Serves 4
Preparation time 10 minutes
Cooking time 8-10 minutes

1 Wash the squid and pat it dry. Cut the tubular part into ½-inch (1-cm) rings. Cut the tentacles into 2 or 3 pieces.
2 Heat the oil in a medium skillet over a medium-high heat. Add the garlic and onion. Turn down the heat to medium, stir, and cook for 1 minute. Add the tomatoes, stir, and cook for 2–3 minutes.
3 Turn up the heat to high and add the squid, vinegar, and salt. Stir and cook for 3–4 minutes, or until the squid turns opaque.

1 lb (500 g) squid, cleaned

3 tablespoons olive oil

4 garlic cloves, chopped finely

small (50 g) onion, finely chopped

6 canned plum tomatoes, drained and coarsely chopped

1 teaspoon vinegar

¾ teaspoon salt

Nutritional values per serving

Carbs 7 g

Fat 12 g

Protein 20 g

Kcals 225

Sea Bass with Fennel

This dish is simplicity itself. The fennel imparts a delicate flavor to the fish, which is beautiful if served with a sharp-tasting salad such as orange and arugula.

Serves 4
Preparation time 2 minutes
Cooking time 20–30 minutes

1 Make 3 diagonal deep slits on each side of the fish. Season the cavities well, then insert a fennel sprig into each slit. Brush the fish well with olive oil.
2 Cook the fish under a preheated medium broiler or on top of a charcoal barbecue for 10–15 minutes on each side, basting occasionally with olive oil. Serve with lemon wedges.

4 medium sea bass, weighing about 2 lb (1 kg) in total, scaled and gutted

6 sprigs fresh fennel

4 tablespoons olive oil, plus extra for basting

salt and pepper

lemon wedges, to serve

Nutritional values per serving

Carbs 0 g

Fat 20 g

Protein 48 g

Kcals 380

Halibut in Caper and White Wine Sauce

If you buy the fish the day before you cook it, make sure you take it out of its wrapping and keep it on a covered plate in the fridge. It will taste much fresher.

Serves 4
Preparation time 5 minutes
Cooking time 20 minutes

1¾ lb (875 g) halibut, cut into 1-inch (2.5-cm) thick slices

12 tablespoons olive oil

3 medium onions, finely chopped

2 tablespoons capers

3 tablespoons chopped parsley

12 tablespoons dry white wine

salt and pepper

1 Wash the halibut in cold water and pat dry.

2 Heat half the olive oil in a large skillet over a medium heat. Sprinkle the fish slices with a little salt and place in the hot oil. Cook for about 5 minutes on each side. Remove the skillet from the heat and drain off most of the oil.

3 Put the remaining oil in a separate small saucepan. Add the chopped onion and fry over a medium heat until lightly colored. Add the capers, chopped parsley, and a pinch of salt. Cook, stirring frequently with a wooden spoon and mashing the capers into the sauce.

4 Add the white wine, bring to a boil, and reduce by half.

5 Pour the sauce on top of the fish, basting over a medium heat for a few minutes, until heated through.

6 Transfer the fish to a serving dish, pour over the remaining sauce, and sprinkle with black pepper. Ideal served with broccoli and a small portion of brown rice.

Nutritional values per serving

Carbs 6.2 g

Fat 27 g

Protein 50 g

Kcals 504

Broiled Fillet of Mackerel with Apple Chutney

Spicy apple chutney cuts through the rich taste of the mackerel, making this a great lunch or supper dish. It could also be an interesting winter appetizer. To complement the powerful, spicy flavors, serve the fish with steamed green vegetables or a green salad.

Serves 4
Preparation time 5 minutes
Cooking time 30 minutes

1 Lightly brush the mackerel fillets with oil and sprinkle with the cayenne and thyme. Place on a broiler rack.

2 To make the chutney, sweat the onion with all the spices, garlic, and a little oil in a stainless-steel saucepan for 2 minutes over a medium heat.

3 Add the apples to the saucepan, together with the rest of the chutney ingredients, and simmer over a low heat for 20 minutes.

4 Broil the mackerel fillets under a hot broiler for 8 minutes until golden brown. Serve with the warm chutney and a wedge of lime.

4 mackerel, weighing 8 oz (250 g) each, filleted and boned

oil for broiling

½ teaspoon cayenne pepper

½ teaspoon thyme

2 limes, cut into wedges

For the chutney

1 small onion, finely chopped

a pinch of ground cumin

a pinch of cumin seeds

a pinch of ground ginger

a pinch of turmeric

a pinch of chili powder

1 garlic clove, finely chopped

oil for frying

8 oz (250 g) cooking apples, peeled and roughly chopped

2 tablespoons cider vinegar

2 tablespoons honey

1 teaspoon hazelnut oil

Nutritional values per serving

Carbs 13 g

Fat 44 g

Protein 52 g

Kcals 663

Shrimp and Cucumber Curry

The fiery spices in this unusual curry are tempered beautifully by the delicate taste of the shrimp and the cucumber. Scallops will work just as well, and try using scallions instead of regular, for a bit of variety.

Serves 4
Preparation time 5 minutes
Cooking time 18 minutes

1 In a medium saucepan, combine the chopped onions, chopped garlic, coriander, ground fennel, white pepper, cumin, turmeric, and water. Crumble in the red chilies, then stir thoroughly. Bring to a boil and boil, uncovered, for 5 minutes.
2 Add the cucumber to the saucepan and simmer for 5 minutes, then add the shrimp, salt, and sugar.
3 Reduce the heat to simmering point and cook for 1 minute. Add the coconut milk and return to a boil. Lower the heat again and simmer for 1 minute, stirring continually. Remove the saucepan from the heat.
4 Put the oil in a small skillet, heat, and add the sliced garlic and onions. Cook until golden. Add the fennel seeds, stir once, and then pour the garlic and onions into the pan containing the curry.
5 Cover immediately to seal the aromas and serve with a small portion of rice and a side dish of vegetables.

1 medium-sized (125 g) onion—¾ of it finely chopped and ¼ finely sliced

6 garlic cloves, 4 finely chopped and 2 finely sliced

2 tablespoons ground coriander

1 tablespoon ground fennel

1 teaspoon ground white pepper

1 tablespoon ground cumin

1 teaspoon ground turmeric

2 cups (450 ml) water

3–4 dried hot chilies

8-inch (300 g) cucumber, peeled and thickly sliced

12 oz (375 g) raw shrimp, peeled and deveined

¾ teaspoon salt

¾ teaspoon sugar

1⅔ cups (400 ml) coconut milk

2 tablespoons vegetable oil

1 teaspoon whole fennel seeds

Nutritional values per serving
Carbs 12.5 g
Fat 8.5 g
Protein 18 g
Kcals 203

Mussels with Chorizo

This unusual combination is an utter delight, as the smokiness of the chorizo sausage marries perfectly with the mussels, giving the dish a hearty quality. Even though the cooking time is quite short, it may take you a while to clean and scrub the mussels, but the end result is worth the extra effort. The sauce is so delicious you may want to allow yourself a little bread or a small portion of rice to soak it up. It's also great with a large salad.

Serves 4
Preparation time 20 minutes
Cooking time 20 minutes

4 lb (2 kg) mussels

½ cup (125 ml) white wine

1 tablespoon olive oil

1 onion, finely chopped

3 garlic cloves, finely chopped

11 oz (325 g) chorizo sausage, finely sliced

2 teaspoons tomato paste

3 tomatoes, skinned and finely chopped

1 bouquet garni

a few saffron strands

2 tablespoons chopped parsley

salt and pepper

1 Scrub the mussels thoroughly, removing the beards and discarding any mussels that stay open when tapped.

2 Place the wine in a large saucepan and bring to a boil. Add the mussels and cover the pan. Cook briskly for 2–3 minutes, or until the mussels open. Strain the mussels, reserving the liquid. Discard any that haven't opened.

3 Heat the oil in the same saucepan and fry the onion until it turns golden. Add the garlic and cook for 1 minute. Add the chorizo and cook over a medium heat for 3-4 minutes.

4 Add the tomato paste, then blend in the reserved cooking liquid. Add the tomatoes, bouquet garni, and saffron. Season with salt and pepper. Bring to a boil and cook, uncovered for 10 minutes so the liquor reduces slightly.

5 Add the mussels and parsley to the saucepan and reheat gently for about 1 minute.

6 Serve with salad and bread or rice if desired.

Nutritional values per serving
Carbs 10 g
Fat 27 g
Protein 39 g
Kcals 460

Tamarind and Lemon Grass Beef

This is the type of food that is tossed together in minutes at street stalls all over Thailand. The meat is seared, juicy, and never overcooked. Vegetables remain crisp, retaining the majority of their immune-boosting phyto-nutrients.

Serves 4
Preparation time 15 minutes
Cooking time 12 minutes

1 Heat the oil over high heat in a wok or skillet. Toss in the meat and cook for 2–3 minutes.

2 Add the lemon grass, shallots, and chilies, and stir-fry for a further 5 minutes, or until the meat is well browned.

3 Add the tamarind, lime juice, fish sauce, sugar, and papaya, and stir-fry for a further 4 minutes.

4 Serve with a little coconut rice and salad.

1 tablespoon olive oil

500 g (1 lb) lean beefsteak, cut into strips

2 stalks lemon grass, chopped

6 shallots, chopped

2 green chilies, chopped

3 tablespoons tamarind paste

2 tablespoons lime juice

2 teaspoons fish sauce

2 teaspoons brown sugar

7 oz (200 g) green papaya, peeled and shredded

Nutritional values per serving
Carbs 13.5 g
Fat 10 g
Protein 28 g
Kcals 265

Veal with Wine and Lemon

There's no need for lengthy stewing and we certainly don't want breaded escalopes. Try this fresh twist on veal instead. It is light and just as good with a summer salad as it is with a pile of steamed vegetables and a few new potatoes.

Serves 4
Preparation time 5 minutes
Cooking time 30–35 minutes

1 Heat the oil in a skillet over a high heat, then add the meat to the skillet and brown evenly. Remove from the pan with a slotted spoon and set aside.

2 Add the onion and garlic to the skillet and cook over medium heat until golden.

3 Add the fennel and fry for a further 3–4 minutes, or until softened.

4 Return the veal to the skillet and add the wine, stock, lemon zest, bay leaves, and thyme. Bring to a boil and boil for 5 minutes.

5 Turn down the heat and simmer, covered, for a further 20–25 minutes. Season and serve with vegetables or a small portion of brown rice.

2 tablespoons olive oil

2 lb (1 kg) veal, chopped into cubes

2 onions, sliced

4 garlic cloves, sliced

2 baby fennel bulbs, roughly chopped

2 cups (475 ml) white wine

2 cups (475 ml) chicken stock

zest of ½ a lemon, cut into julienne strips (matchsticks)

4 bay leaves

1 tablespoon thyme

salt and pepper

Nutritional values per serving
Carbs 6.5 g
Fat 12 g
Protein 58 g
Kcals 368

Calves' Liver and Sage

This classic combination is delicious and takes just minutes to cook—in fact the secret is not to cook it too much as it can become very dry. If you want to be thoroughly dedicated to the low-carb quest, serve with vegetables, but if you want to misbehave, a small portion of creamed potatoes soaks up the sauce beautifully.

Serves 4
Preparation time 5 minutes
Cooking time 5 minutes

1 Season the flour with salt and pepper and coat the liver.

2 Heat the oil and butter in a large skillet, add the garlic and liver, and fry quickly for 1–2 minutes on each side.

3 Add the sage and the stock, and cook for 2 minutes. Remove the liver from the skillet and keep it warm on a serving dish while you finish the sauce.

4 Add the Marsala to the skillet and season with salt and pepper. Bring the sauce to a boil, stirring continuously for 1 minute, then pour over the liver and garnish with sage to serve.

1 tablespoon rice flour

1 lb (500 g) calves' liver, thinly sliced

1 tablespoon olive oil

2 tablespoons (25 g) butter

1 garlic clove, chopped

2 teaspoons chopped sage

½ cup (125 ml) chicken stock

3 tablespoons Marsala

salt and pepper

sage sprigs, to garnish

Nutritional values per serving

Carbs 4.2 g

Fat 8 g

Protein 23 g

Kcals 195

Bursa Kebabs

This recipe originates from Bursa, in Turkey. The flavor of the kebabs is greatly enhanced if the lamb is left to marinate overnight in the refrigerator. They make an extremely quick meal when you're in a hurry as the cooking time is so short.

Serves 4
Preparation time 5 minutes
Cooking time 6–8 minutes, plus marinating time

4 tablespoons olive oil

½ onion, finely chopped

½ teaspoon ground cumin

1 lb (500 g) boneless lamb, cut into large chunks

8 oz (250 g) tomatoes, skinned and finely chopped

1 cup (250 g) plain strained yogurt

salt and pepper

To garnish

1 green bell pepper, cored, seeded, and sliced

2 tablespoons chopped parsley

1 Mix the oil, onion, and cumin together, then season with salt and pepper. Add the lamb and marinate in the refrigerator for a minimum of 2 hours and preferably overnight.

2 When ready to cook, remove the lamb from the dish and reserve the marinade. Thread the lamb onto skewers and broil under a high heat for 6–8 minutes, turning once or twice to ensure even cooking.

3 Meanwhile, heat the reserved marinade in a saucepan and cook for about 2–3 minutes over a medium heat, or until the onions have softened.

4 Add the tomatoes to the saucepan and cook for a further 3 minutes, stirring occasionally.

5 Remove the meat from the skewers and place on a warmed serving dish. Pour over the tomato mixture and add a dollop of yogurt. Garnish with the green bell pepper and parsley, and serve immediately with a green salad and a whole-wheat pita bread, if desired.

Nutritional values per serving

Carbs 7.7 g

Fat 30 g

Protein 29 g

Kcals 419

Marinated Pork Tenderloin

This is an incredibly simple dish to make, and is perfect with Chinese greens or bok choy. Marinate the pork in the refrigerator overnight for an even tastier, quicker option and as an effortless main course for a dinner party.

Serves 4
Preparation time 5 minutes
Cooking time 20 minutes, plus marinating time

1 Mix the marinade ingredients together, then place the pork tederloin in a shallow dish and cover evenly with the marinade. Leave for at least 2–3 hours, and preferably overnight.

2 When you are ready to cook the meat, preheat the oven to 350°F.

3 Drain the pork, reserving the marinade. Lay the pork in the linseeds on both sides so it is evenly covered.

4 Put the meat on a roasting pan and seal it over a high heat on the stove. Then put it in the oven to roast for 18–20 minutes, or until golden brown.

5 Meanwhile, remove the cinnamon stick from the marinade and pour the liquid into a nonstick saucepan. Add the white wine and bring to a boil. Reduce the heat and simmer until it has the consistency of a sticky glaze. Remove from the heat and set aside.

6 Remove the pork from the oven and cut into ¼-inch (5-mm) slices. Serve on a bed of steamed vegetables, such as bok choy or spinach, and drizzle the glaze over the pork.

2 pieces of pork tenderloin weighing 8 oz (250 g) each

1 tablespoon linseeds (flaxseeds)

⅔ cup (150 ml) dry white wine

For the marinade

1 stick cinnamon

2 tablespoons soy sauce

2 garlic cloves, crushed

1 teaspoon grated fresh ginger root

1 tablespoon honey

1 teaspoon crushed coriander seeds

1 teaspoon sesame oil

Nutritional values per serving

Carbs 5.8 g

Fat 11.5 g

Protein 28 g

Kcals 265

Mustard Lamb Loin

Tender pink lamb with garlic is a match made in heaven. Add to this a fiery blast of mustard and some fresh herbs, and instantly you have a dinner-party dish to impress.

Serves 4
Preparation time 5 minutes
Cooking time 15 minutes

1 Trim the lamb of any fat. Preheat the oven to 400°F.

2 In a bowl, mix together the garlic, mustard, mint, cilantro, and oil until well combined.

3 Rub the lamb with the garlic and mustard mixture and place it in a baking dish.

4 Bake in the oven for around 10–15 minutes, or until the lamb is cooked to your liking. Allow the meat to stand for 10 minutes and serve with a selection of steamed vegetables.

1 lb (500 g) boneless lamb loin

4 garlic cloves, crushed

2 tablespoon Dijon or English mustard

2 tablespoons chopped mint

1 tablespoon chopped cilantro

1 tablespoon olive oil

Nutritional values per serving

Carbs 1.6 g

Fat 37 g

Protein 21 g

Kcals 420

Rapid-fire Ribs

Don't faint at the quantity of pork ribs—remember, the bulk of the weight is the bone. These are especially good if you can throw together the marinade the day before and leave the ribs to marinate overnight in the fridge. Then it takes only 25 minutes for the spicy feast to cook through.

Serves 4
Preparation time 5 minutes
Cooking time 35 minutes, plus marinating time

1 First, mix the marinade ingredients together in a bowl that is large enough to hold all the ribs and combine well.

2 Toss the ribs in the marinade and place in the refrigerator for at least 2–3 hours and preferably overnight.

3 When you are ready to cook, preheat the oven to 425°F.

4 Put the oil in a large skillet and sear the ribs, a few at a time, until browned. Transfer the ribs to a roasting pan and bake in the oven for 25 minutes.

5 To serve, toss the ribs with the cilantro leaves and green onions, and provide a selection of dips and salad.

4 lb (2 kg) pork ribs

2 tablespoons olive oil

For the marinade

2 tablespoons sherry

2 tablespoons honey

2 tablespoons light soy sauce

2 teaspoons sesame oil

1¼ cups (300 ml) tomato paste

½ teaspoon five spice powder

1 teaspoon ground coriander seeds

1 teaspoon minced red chilies

To serve

2 tablespoons chopped cilantro leaves

2 tablespoons chopped green onions

Quick&Easy Tip

You can also put these ribs on the barbecue where they will cook in the same amount of time.

Nutritional values per serving

Carbs 11 g

Fat 50 g

Protein 48 g

Kcals 745

Seared Steak with Parmesan and Arugula

When the mood for red meat hits you, only a steak will do. With plenty of red onions and the classic combination of arugula and Parmesan, you won't even miss the French fries—honest!

Serves 4
Preparation time 10 minutes
Cooking time 7–8 minutes

3 tablespoons olive oil

2 red onions, thickly sliced

1 lb (500 g) sirloin steak, cut into 8 steaks

8 cups (150 g) arugula

1½ cups (125 g) Parmesan shavings

3 tablespoons flat-leaf parsley

2 tablespoons balsamic vinegar

black pepper

1 Heat 1 tablespoon of the olive oil in a skillet over a medium heat. Add the onions and cook for 5 minutes, or until golden. Remove the onions from the skillet and set aside.

2 Increase the heat to high and add the steaks to the skillet. Cook for about 30 seconds—1 minute on each side, or until sealed and seared.

3 Toss together the arugula, Parmesan, parsley, balsamic vinegar, black pepper, and the remaining olive oil.

4 To serve, place a steak on each serving plate, add some of the salad mixture, then another steak, and top with fried onions.

Nutritional values per serving

Carbs 6.7 g

Fat 17 g

Protein 31 g

Kcals 308

Pork with Chinese Cabbage

Stir-frying has to be one of the quickest and easiest methods of cooking healthy low-carb ingredients. This dish is a meal in itself, but try serving it on a bed of crunchy bean sprouts.

Serves 4
Preparation time 5 minutes
Cooking time 40 minutes

1 Toast the sesame seeds in a dry skillet over a medium heat for 1–2 minutes, or until golden brown, shaking continuously. Remove to a cool plate and set aside.

2 Mix together the garlic, green onions, and cayenne pepper, then mix with the pork, making sure the meat and flavorings are well combined.

3 Heat the oils in a skillet and stir-fry the pork over a high heat, in about 3 batches, cooking for about 5 minutes on each side until golden and cooked through. Remove the meat from the pan and set aside.

4 Add the soy sauce, honey, and cabbage to the pan and toss to mix. Cover and cook over a medium heat for 5–6 minutes.

5 Return the pork to the pan, add the reserved sesame seeds, toss well, and serve immediately.

1 tablespoon white sesame seeds

2 garlic cloves, very finely sliced

3 green onions, sliced diagonally into ¾-inch (2-cm) pieces

½ teaspoon cayenne pepper

10 oz (300 g) pork loin, cut into thick strips

2 tablespoons olive oil

2 teaspoons sesame oil

2 tablespoons soy sauce

2 teaspoons honey

13 oz (400 g) Savoy cabbage, cut into strips

Nutritional values per serving
Carbs 8 g
Fat 28 g
Protein 18 g
Kcals 360

Wild Venison Steaks with Ratatouille

Venison is a fantastic source of lean protein. Despite being low in fat, it has a beautiful flavor that is greatly enhanced by the fresh-tasting ratatouille, which has the additional benefit of being full of low-GI vegetables.

Serves 4
Preparation time 15 minutes
Cooking time 16 minutes

1 Sandwich the venison steaks between sheets of waxed paper, then roll with a rolling pin to flatten them.

2 Season with some salt and freshly ground black pepper and rub in 1 tablespoon of the olive oil.

3 Heat the rest of the oil in a deep skillet and add the garlic, red onion, and green onions. Stir-fry over a medium-high heat for 2 minutes, then add the rest of the ingredients, except the venison. Cook over a medium heat for about 14 minutes.

4 Meanwhile, broil the steaks for 3–5 minutes on each side, depending on how well done you like them. Wrap each steak in foil and allow to stand for 2–4 minutes.

5 Serve the steaks over a mound of ratatouille and garnish with freshly chopped parsley.

4 venison steaks weighing 4 oz (125 g) each

2 tablespoons olive oil

1 garlic clove, crushed

1 medium red onion, chopped

4 green onions, sliced

1 yellow or red bell pepper, seeded and chopped

2 small zucchini, finely sliced

1 small eggplant, cut into 1-inch (2.5-cm) cubes

6 small firm tomatoes, chopped

¼ cup (25 g) walnuts or almonds, chopped

2 tablespoons balsamic vinegar

salt and pepper

flat-leaf parsley, to garnish

Nutritional values per serving
Carbs 11 g
Fat 14 g
Protein 25 g
Kcals 271

Eggplant Gateau

This takes 30 minutes to prepare and can be left in the fridge overnight. It is gorgeous with a great big dollop of hummus and a scattering of fresh herbs.

Serves 4
Preparation time 30 minutes
Cooking time 20 minutes

1 Cover the eggplant slices in lemon juice.
2 To make the sauce, sauté the tomatoes and onions in half of the olive oil in a heavy skillet for 1–2 minutes. Add the tomato paste, white wine, vegetable stock, and herbs. Cook for 10 minutes and puree in a blender.
3 Sauté all the Provençale vegetables in the rest of the oil for 3 minutes over a medium heat. Bind with a little of the tomato sauce and set aside.
4 In a separate skillet fry the eggplant slices in a little oil. Lightly brown each side and drain on paper towels.
5 Next make the gateau. Beginning with the eggplant slices, layer the Provençale mix with the eggplant in a pie pan. Cover with waxed paper or plastic wrap and press down with a heavy weight or dish filled with cold water. Refrigerate for a minimum of 30 minutes or overnight.
6 To serve, cut into wedges, drizzle with sauce, and garnish with pine nuts.

1 eggplant, cut into ¼-inch (5-mm) slices

juice of 1 lemon

4 teaspoons olive oil

2 tablespoons (25 g) roasted pine nuts, to garnish

For the Provençale vegetables

1 zucchini, cut into ½-inch (1-cm) dice

1 red bell pepper, seeded and finely chopped

1 green bell pepper, seeded finely chopped

1 yellow bell pepper, seeded and finely chopped

1 medium-sized onion, finely chopped

4 garlic cloves, roughly chopped

For the sauce

2 beefsteak tomatoes, quartered

1 small onion, roughly chopped

4 teaspoons olive oil

2 teaspoons tomato paste

¼ cup (50 ml) white wine

1¼ cups (300 ml) vegetable stock

1 tablespoon chopped basil

1 thyme sprig

Nutritional values per serving
Carbs 19 g
Fat 15 g
Protein 5.5 g
Kcals 240

Zucchini with Corn, Green Onions, and Parmesan

This is a tasty way to serve zucchini. You can vary the cheese—a nice blue cheese such as Stilton would work—and, if you are a meat-eater, a little chopped ham in place of the corn not only tastes great but brings the carb levels down too.

Serves 2
Preparation time 10 minutes
Cooking time 30 minutes

1 Preheat the oven to 350°F. Cook the zucchini in boiling water for about 5 minutes. Drain, then cut them in half lengthwise and scoop out some of the flesh, leaving a good-sized shell. Chop the flesh and drain to remove any liquid.

2 Mix the zucchini flesh with the corn, green onions, egg yolks, cayenne, and half the Parmesan. Season with a little salt and mix again.

3 Whisk the egg whites until stiff and carefully fold into the zucchini mixture.

4 Place the zucchini shells in an ovenproof dish, spoon in the filling, and sprinkle with the remaining cheese.

5 Cook in the oven for 25 minutes, or until risen. Serve immediately.

6 zucchini

1 cup (150 g) frozen corn

7 oz (200 g) green onions, finely chopped

2 eggs, separated

a pinch of cayenne pepper

½ cup (50 g) grated Parmesan

salt

Nutritional values per serving
Carbs 22 g
Fat 17 g
Protein 29 g
Kcals 345

Gado Gado (Indonesian Vegetables with Peanut Dressing)

The vegetables in this dish can be varied according to what you have available, but whatever you choose, the addition of the spicy peanut sauce will make it a meal to remember. You can prepare this a few hours ahead of time, but don't pour on the dressing until you are ready to serve.

Serves 4
Preparation time 15–20 minutes
Cooking time 25 minutes

6 oz (175 g) green beans, sliced into 2-inch (5-cm) lengths

6 oz (175 g) cauliflower, divided into florets

6 oz (175 g) broccoli, divided into florets

6 oz (175 g) cabbage, cut into fine shreds

3 hard-cooked eggs, quartered

2 large tomatoes, quartered

1 large orange bell pepper, seeded and cut into thin slices

4-inch piece of cucumber (about 150 g), peeled and cut into chunky slices

1 cup (125 g) bean sprouts

For the dressing

2 cups (450 ml) chicken or vegetable stock

½ cup (125 g) crunchy peanut butter

2 garlic cloves, finely chopped

1 green onion, finely chopped

½ teaspoon chili powder

1 tablespoon fish sauce

5 teaspoons fresh lime juice

To garnish

2 green onions, cut into fine slices

2 tablespoons chopped cilantro

Nutritional values per serving

Carbs 16 g

Fat 19 g

Protein 17 g

Kcals 305

1 Bring a medium saucepan of water to a boil, add a little salt, and keep at a gentle boil over a medium-high heat. Add the green beans and boil for 3 minutes, or until they are just tender. Remove with a slotted spoon, place in a colander, and refresh under cold running water. Set aside on a large serving plate.

2 Cook the cauliflower and broccoli for 2–3 minutes and refresh in the same way. Arrange in separate piles on the serving dish. Finally, cook the cabbage strips for 1 minute, drain, and refresh under cold water. Add to the plate.

3 Arrange piles of egg, tomatoes, bell pepper, cucumber, and bean sprouts on the plate. Cover with plastic wrap and set aside.

4 Make the sauce by warming the stock in a saucepan until nearly boiling. Remove from the heat and place the peanut butter in another pan with the garlic, green onion, and chili powder. Gradually add the warm stock to the mixture, stirring continuously until thoroughly blended.

5 Add the fish sauce and lime juice to the saucepan and bring to a boil. Turn down the heat to medium-low and simmer for 15 minutes, stirring occasionally. The sauce should now have thickened to a creamy consistency.

6 Allow to cool slightly and, when ready to serve, pour the warmed dressing over the vegetables and garnish with the chopped green onions and cilantro.

Baked Celeriac and Blue Cheese

This vegetable is great served with roast meat but can easily provide the basis of a vegetarian supper dish if served with a side salad or few steamed vegetables.

Serves 4
Preparation time 5 minutes
Cooking time 35–40 minutes

1 Preheat the oven to 400°F.

2 Place the celeriac in saucepan of salted water and boil for 10 minutes until slightly softened, then drain and set aside to cool slightly.

3 Grease an ovenproof dish with a little butter and layer in the celeriac and hazelnuts. Pour over the cream and bake for 15 minutes.

4 Remove the dish from the oven and sprinkle over the cheese and caraway seeds. Season with pepper and return to the oven for a further 10–15 minutes, or until the cheese is golden.

5 Garnish with a little parsley and serve.

2 lb (1 kg) celeriac, peeled and sliced

1 cup (100 g) chopped roasted hazelnuts

2¼ cups (500 ml) light cream

5 oz (150 g) blue cheese, crumbled

1 teaspoon caraway seeds

salt and black pepper

parsley, to garnish

Nutritional values per serving

Carbs 12 g

Fat 50 g

Protein 17 g

Kcals 580

Quick Chickpea Casserole

In the West we neglect the great garbanzo, commonly known as the chickpea, whereas in the Middle East this humble legume is a staple ingredient at mealtimes. It is always worth having a few cans in the cupboard as dried chickpeas mean overnight soaking and at least 1½ hours' cooking time.

Serves 6
Preparation time 5 minutes
Cooking time 30 minutes

2 large onions, chopped

4 tablespoons olive oil

1–2 tablespoons ground cumin

4–5 garlic cloves, chopped

2 x 13-oz (400-g) cans chickpeas, drained

1¼ cups (300 ml) vegetable stock

juice of 1 lemon

1 lb (500 g) fresh spinach, roughly chopped

salt and pepper

1 Sauté the onions in the oil in a large saucepan over a medium heat until softened. Add the cumin and garlic, stir, and cook for 1 minute.

2 Add the chickpeas, vegetable stock, and the lemon juice. Cover and simmer for 20 minutes.

3 Add the spinach and season with salt and pepper. Mix well and cook for another 7 minutes.

4 Serve hot, at room temperature or cold. The flavor improves if the casserole is left overnight.

Nutritional values per serving

Carbs 29 g

Fat 14 g

Protein 13 g

Kcals 286

Green Risotto

This creamy risotto is satisfying and extra cheesy thanks to the addition of blue cheese as well as Parmesan. Despite this, it retains a low-carb status by keeping the rice content low and the vegetable content high.

Serves 6
Preparation time 10 minutes
Cooking time 25 minutes

1 Put the butter in a heavy saucepan, add the garlic, and cook over a medium heat until golden. Meanwhile, heat the stock in a separate saucepan.

2 Add the rice to the pan containing the garlic and toss together to coat the grains in the butter.

3 Stir and add ½ cup (125 ml) of the hot stock to the saucepan with the rice. Stir until it has been absorbed—about 5 minutes—then add another ½ cup (125 ml). Repeat until the rice is nearly tender. The consistency will be quite liquid at this point.

4 Add the cream, beans, and asparagus. Continue cooking until the rice is al dente, then stir in the blue cheese, Parmesan, and basil.

5 Season with salt and pepper, and serve immediately.

1 tablespoon butter

3 garlic cloves, chopped

4½ cups (1 liter) vegetable broth

8 oz (250 g) Arborio rice

⅓ cup (75 ml) light cream

8 oz (250 g) green beans, blanched and cut into bite-sized pieces

16 7-inch long (about 250 g) asparagus spears, blanched and cut into bite-sized pieces

4 oz (125 g) blue cheese (such as Roquefort, Gorgonzola, or Danish Blue)

4–6 tablespoons coarsely grated Parmesan

⅓ cup (15 g) basil, coarsely chopped

salt and pepper

Nutritional values per serving

Carbs 40 g

Fat 20 g

Protein 14 g

Kcals 395

Spicy Eggplant and Tofu

This dish is wonderful served hot or cold, and the amount of chili can be varied according to taste. Make sure you use cilantro stalks and not just the leaves, as the stalks and roots have a very intense flavor that is perfect for this dish. Also try using fresh mint instead of basil as a final touch.

Serves 4
Preparation time 10 minutes
Cooking time 10 minutes

1 Using a food processor or blender, blend the chilies, garlic, cilantro stalks, onion, sugar, lime juice, and fish sauce to make a smooth paste.

2 Heat the oil in a large skillet or wok, add the paste, and stir over a high heat for 1 minute, or until fragrant.

3 Add the eggplant, stir to combine, and cook for 4–5 minutes or until just soft.

4 Add the tofu and half the basil and dried shrimp, if using. Heat through for 2–3 minutes.

5 Garnish with the remaining basil and serve.

2–4 small fresh red or green chilies

4 garlic cloves, crushed

4 cilantro stalks, chopped

1 small onion, chopped

1 teaspoon soft brown sugar

2 tablespoons lime juice

2 tablespoons fish sauce

1 tablespoon oil

13 oz (400 g) baby eggplant, sliced in ¾-inch (2-cm) slices

8 oz (250 g) firm tofu, cut into 1½-inch (3.5-cm) cubes

⅓ cup (15 g) Thai basil

2 teaspoons dried shrimp, finely chopped (optional)

Nutritional values per serving

Carbs 6 g

Fat 7 g

Protein 9 g

Kcals 120

Veggie Chili

The great thing about this throw-it-all-in-a-pot dish is that it tastes even better the next day, when all the flavors have infused—and it's quick to make too. If you want to give it more body and raise the protein content, add some cubed silken tofu or ground Quorn.

Serves 8
Preparation time 15 minutes
Cooking time 30 minutes

3 tablespoons olive oil

3 onions, chopped

4 garlic cloves, chopped

1 large green bell pepper, seeded and chopped

1 large red bell pepper, seeded and chopped

2 tablespoons mild chili powder

2 tablespoons paprika

1 tablespoon ground cumin

1 bay leaf

2 teaspoons dried oregano

1 lb (500 g) fresh or canned tomatoes, chopped

3¼ cups (750 ml) vegetable stock

1½ cups (375 g) canned kidney or borlotti beans, drained

salt and pepper

To garnish

cheese, grated

lettuce, finely sliced

onion, finely chopped

avocado, diced

hot pepper sauce

sour cream

1 Heat the oil in a large skillet, then sauté the onions, garlic, and red and green bell peppers over a medium heat for 2–3 minutes.

2 Add the chili powder, paprika, and cumin to the skillet and cook for 1 minute.

3 Put all the other ingredients into the skillet (add the tofu or Quorn if using), bring to a boil, and turn the heat down to a simmer.

4 Cook uncovered for 20–25 minutes, or until the chili has thickened.

5 Season with salt and pepper and serve with a selection of garnishes.

Nutritional values per serving

Carbs 33 g

Fat 12 g

Protein 9.7 g

Kcals 273

Pea, Egg, and Tofu Curry

As the eggs will be cooked further in the curry, simply put them into boiling water for 4–5 minutes, plunge them into cold water for about 5 minutes, and then peel. This meal is comfort food, so throw a few logs on the fire before you start to eat and snuggle up for the evening.

Serves 4
Preparation time 5 minutes
Cooking time 25 minutes

1 Begin by coating the eggs in the turmeric.

2 Heat the oil in a large skillet and lightly fry the eggs over a moderate heat for 2 minutes, then set aside.

3 Add the bay leaf, onion, and garlic, and cook over medium heat for 2 minutes. Add the cilantro, garam masala, and chili powder, and cook for 1 minute more.

4 Add the tomato paste, tomatoes, and water. Cover and cook for 5 minutes.

5 Return the eggs to the skillet with the tofu, yogurt, and peas. Season with a little salt and pepper.

6 Cook for 5 minutes, then remove the bay leaf, sprinkle with the cilantro, and serve.

4 hard-cooked eggs, peeled

½ teaspoon turmeric

3 tablespoons vegetable oil

1 bay leaf

2 onions, finely chopped

2 garlic cloves, finely chopped

1½ teaspoons ground coriander

1½ teaspoons ground garam masala

½ teaspoon chili powder

1 tablespoon tomato paste

2 medium-sized (125 g) canned tomatoes, chopped

½ cup (125 ml) water

4 oz (125 g) tofu, cut into ½-inch (1-cm) cubes

1 tablespoon plain yogurt

1 cup (100 g) frozen peas

2 tablespoons cilantro, finely chopped

salt and pepper

Nutritional values per serving
Carbs 10 g
Fat 18 g
Protein 12 g
Kcals 257

Mushroom and Artichoke Bake

This is a great supper dish, especially when served with a large, peppery green salad. It will also work as a great potato substitute to serve with a roast. Vary by using eggplant or red bell peppers in place of the mushrooms.

Serves 2
Preparation time 5 minutes
Cooking time 25 minutes

1 lb (500 g) artichoke hearts, drained

1 teaspoon olive oil

small onion, finely chopped

2 garlic cloves, finely chopped

10 oz (300 g) mushrooms, sliced

1 tablespoon basil, chopped

1 tablespoon oregano

1 tablespoon lemon juice

1 tablespoon dry white wine

1 tablespoon brown breadcrumbs

1 tablespoon grated Parmesan

salt and pepper

parsley sprigs, to serve

1 Preheat the oven to 350°F.

2 Place the artichokes in a lightly oiled medium-sized roasting pan.

3 Heat the oil in a medium-sized nonstick skillet over moderate heat. Add the onion and garlic, and fry gently, stirring frequently, for 3 minutes. Add the mushrooms and fresh herbs.

4 Add the lemon juice and wine, then season and cook for a further 3 minutes. Remove from heat and stir in the breadcrumbs.

5 Spoon the mushroom mixture evenly over the artichokes, then bake in the oven, uncovered, for 10 minutes.

6 Remove from the oven and sprinkle over the Parmesan. Bake for another 10 minutes, then garnish with fresh parsley and serve.

Nutritional values per serving

Carbs 14 g

Fat 7 g

Protein 14 g

Kcals 168

Quick Tagine of Red Onions

This dish is great with red meats and cold cuts or served alongside less robustly flavored vegetarian dishes. Add cherry tomatoes for a great variation and melt chunks of goat cheese for a hearty main-meal option.

Serves 6
Preparation time 1–2 minutes
Cooking time 30 minutes

1 Preheat the oven to 400°F.
2 Heat the oil in a skillet Add the onions, saffron, ginger, pepper, cinnamon, and sugar, and cook over a high heat for 2–3 minutes, stirring continuously.
3 Add the red wine to the skillet, continuing to stir, and boil rapidly until reduced to a syrupy consistency.
4 Transfer the onion mixture to a heavy casserole dish and cover with foil. Place in the oven and cook for 20 minutes.
5 Remove from the oven and take off the foil, then cook for a further 5 minutes, or until the onions are lightly glazed. Sprinkle with a little fresh parsley or cilantro and serve hot or cold.

1½ lb (750 g) red onions, finely sliced

6 tablespoons olive oil

a pinch of saffron

¼ teaspoon ground ginger

1 teaspoon ground black pepper

½ teaspoon ground cinnamon

1 tablespoon brown sugar

⅔ cups (150 ml) red wine

chopped parsley or cilantro, to serve

Nutritional values per serving

Carbs 9 g

Fat 15.5

Protein 1 g

Kcals 170

Broccoli with Toasted Sesame Seeds

This makes a great accompaniment to chicken dishes and, as broccoli is rich in nutrients and sesame seeds protect against free radicals, it is great for your health too!

Serves 4–6
Preparation time 5 minutes
Cooking time 10 minutes

1 Steam or boil the broccoli for 8–10 minutes, or until tender.
2 Meanwhile, lightly toast the sesame seeds in a dry pan over a low heat until golden brown. Set aside.
3 Place the broccoli in a warmed serving dish and sprinkle with the sesame seeds.

1 lb (500 g) broccoli, cut into florets

3 oz (75 g) sesame seeds

Nutritional values per serving

Carbs 2.35 g

Fat 13 g

Protein 7 g

Kcals 150

Green Beans with Ham and Garlic

This makes an excellent accompaniment to any meal and is great served hot or cold. Replace the ham with finely chopped chorizo sausage for a Spanish-influenced variation, or use fava beans instead of green beans.

Serves 4
Preparation time 5 minutes
Cooking time 15 minutes

1 Cook the beans in boiling salted water for about 8 minutes, until almost tender.
2 Meanwhile, fry the onion in the oil until softened.
3 Add the garlic and ham and cook for 1 minute. Add the drained beans, cover, and cook for 5 minutes.
4 Season with salt and pepper and transfer to a warmed serving dish.

1 lb (500 g) green beans

2 tablespoons olive oil

1 onion, sliced

1 garlic clove, crushed

3-oz (75-g) piece Parma ham, cubed

salt and pepper

Nutritional values per serving

Carbs 7 g

Fat 10.5 g

Protein 8 g

Kcals 155

Cauliflower with Tomato and Herb Sauce

This dish makes a fresh addition to a meal, but to turn it into a vegetarian main meal for 2–3 people, melt some grated cheddar over the finished dish.

2 tablespoons olive oil

3 garlic cloves, peeled and finely chopped

1 tablespoon chopped fresh parsley

1 tablespoon chopped fresh basil

12 oz (375 g) canned plum tomatoes, roughly chopped

1 medium cauliflower weighing about 1 lb (500 g), separated into florets

salt and pepper

Nutritional values per serving

Carbs 8.5 g

Fat 8.7 g

Protein 5.7 g

Kcals 133

Serves 4
Preparation time 5 minutes
Cooking time 25 minutes

1 Heat the oil and sauté the garlic in a large saucepan over a moderate heat until lightly colored.
2 Add the herbs and chopped tomatoes and simmer, uncovered, for 10 minutes.
3 Add the cauliflower florets, season with salt and freshly ground black pepper, and cook for about 12 minutes over a medium heat, or until tender.

Chinese Greens in Oyster Sauce

A great accompaniment to any Asian meat or fish dish. *Choy sum* is flowering Chinese cabbage with pale green stems and a rounded leaf. It can be found in Asian supermarkets.

8 oz (250 g) Chinese broccoli (*gai lan*), cut into short lengths

5 oz (150 g) *choy sum*, cut into short lengths

2 teaspoons sesame oil

1 teaspoon grated ginger root

3 tablespoons oyster sauce

3 tablespoons chicken or vegetable stock

1 tablespoon soy sauce

salt

sesame seeds, to serve

Nutritional values per serving

Carbs 18 g

Fat 13 g

Protein 17 g

Kcals 266

Serves 4
Preparation time 1–2 minutes
Cooking time 5 minutes

1 Blanch the Chinese broccoli and *choy sum* in a pan of salted boiling water for 30 seconds, then drain.
2 Heat the oil in a wok over a high heat, add the ginger root, and cook for 1 minute. Add the remaining ingredients and cook for 2 minutes more, stirring continuously. Cook for 1 minute until heated through.
3 Serve immediately, sprinkled with a few sesame seeds if desired.

Okra with Lime

This dish is fabulous as part of a vegetarian mezze, or as a side dish with some simple broiled fish or meat. Apparently cactus tastes very much like okra so, if you find yourself cooking a low-carb meal in Santa Fe, make the most of the local ingredients!

Serves 8
Preparation time 5 minutes
Cooking time 25–30 minutes

1 Trim off the okra tops and discard. Rinse the okra under cold water and drain.

2 Heat the oil in a large saucepan, add the onion, and sauté until light golden.

3 Add the chilies, garlic, and ground coriander. Sauté for 1–2 minutes and then add the tomatoes with their juice. Once the liquid starts to bubble, add the okra, lime juice, and seasoning.

4 Shake the pan to distribute the ingredients, then cover and cook gently for 20–25 minutes. Add the cilantro and serve.

2 lb (1 kg) okra

3 tablespoons olive oil

1 large onion, finely chopped

1–2 dried chilies, crushed

3 garlic cloves, chopped

1 tablespoon ground coriander seeds

13 oz (400 g) canned tomatoes, chopped

2 tablespoons lime juice

2 tablespoons cilantro leaves, coarsely chopped

salt and pepper

Nutritional values per serving
Carbs 8 g
Fat 1.6 g
Protein 8 g
Kcals 102

Spinach with Raisins and Pine Nuts

Pine nuts and raisins are a popular combination in many Spanish recipes.
With wilted spinach, this is a great snack or main-meal accompaniment.

Serves 4
Preparation time 10 minutes
Cooking time 4 minutes

1 Put the raisins in a bowl with a little boiling water and leave
to soak for 10 minutes, then drain.
2 Fry the pine nuts in the oil until they are beginning to color.
3 Add the spinach and garlic and cook quickly until the spinach
has wilted. Toss in the raisins and season with salt and
pepper. Transfer to a warmed serving dish and serve hot.

⅓ cup (50 g) raisins

1 tablespoon olive oil

2 tablespoons (25 g) pine nuts

1 lb (500 g) young spinach,
trimmed

2 garlic cloves, crushed

salt and pepper

Nutritional values per serving

Carbs 15 g

Fat 8.5 g

Protein 5.5 g

Kcals 152

Pumpkin and Spinach Puree

This is very light but has a robust flavor. It is fantastic with lamb dishes,
such as the Bursa Kebabs on page 77.

Serves 4
Preparation time 5–10 minutes
Cooking time 25 minutes

1 Sauté the garlic briefly in the olive oil in a saucepan over
a medium heat, then add the pumpkin and cumin seeds.
Cook for about 10 minutes until the pumpkin begins to soften.
2 Add the spinach and just under 4 cups (900 ml) of stock. Cook
for about 15 minutes, or until the vegetables are tender.
3 Put the vegetables, cream, and the remaining stock in a food
processor or liquidizer and blend into a smooth puree. Add a
little more stock or water if the consistency is too thick.
4 Season the puree with the curry powder and the salt and
pepper. Serve garnished with a little chopped parsley.

4 garlic cloves, chopped

2 tablespoons olive oil

4⅓ cups (about 500 g)
pumpkin or squash flesh cut
into 1-inch (2.5-cm) cubes

1½ teaspoons cumin seeds

4 cups (125 g) spinach or
chard, cut into thin ribbons

5 cups (1.2 liters) vegetable
stock

½ cup (125 ml) sour cream

1 teaspoon curry powder

salt and pepper

chopped parsley, to garnish

Nutritional values per serving

Carbs 10 g

Fat 14 g

Protein 3 g

Kcals 175

Pepperonata

You can double up on the quantities here as this dish keeps for several days in the refrigerator. Also, it doesn't matter what combination of peppers you use, the more colorful the better.

Serves 4–6
Preparation time 10 minutes
Cooking time 20 minutes

4 tablespoons olive oil

1 onion, sliced

3 bell peppers (red, green, orange, or yellow), cored, seeded, and sliced

2 garlic cloves, crushed

6 tomatoes, skinned and sliced

2 tablespoons chopped fresh parsley

salt and pepper

1 Heat the oil in a heavy saucepan, add the onion, peppers, and garlic, and fry gently for about 15 minutes, stirring occasionally.

2 Add the tomatoes, parsley, and seasoning, and cook for 5 minutes. Leave to cool.

3 Transfer to a large dish to serve.

Nutritional values per serving

Carbs 9 g

Fat 10 g

Protein 1.9 g

Kcals 140

Steamed Asparagus with Lemon and Anchovy Butter

The mildness of fresh asparagus is perfectly complemented by the saltiness of anchovies and the sharpness of fresh lemon. You could use 1 tablespoon of dried shrimp or 2 tablespoons of Thai fish sauce instead depending on your preference. Or maybe you could try one of the flavored butters on page 125.

Serves 4–6
Preparation time 1–2 minutes
Cooking time 4–5 minutes

1 Put the anchovies, butter, chili, and freshly ground black pepper in a food processor and process until smooth. Add lemon juice to taste.

2 Roll the butter into a log and wrap in foil. Refrigerate until needed.

3 Steam the asparagus in a steamer for about 4–5 minutes. Cut the log of butter into ½-in (1-cm) slices.

4 Serve the asparagus immediately, topped with the disks of butter.

10–12 (50 g) anchovies

⅔ cups (150 g) butter

a pinch of dried chili

juice of 1 lemon

2 lb (1 kg) fresh asparagus, trimmed

pepper

Nutritional values per serving

Carbs 1.6 g

Fat 10 g

Protein 3.5 g

Kcals 118

Flourless Chocolate Cake

We all have to push the "bad" button from time to time and, if you have a sweet tooth, this usually involves chocolate. It is hard to believe, but a portion of this cake will add only 20 g of carbs to your daily tally.

Serves 8
Preparation time 1–2 minutes
Cooking time 50 minutes

1 Preheat the oven to 350°F. Line a 9-inch (23-cm) cake pan with parchment paper, making sure you also line the sides of the pan to prevent the cake from sticking.

2 Put the chocolate and butter in a large saucepan and melt gently over a low heat, stirring until smooth.

3 Remove the saucepan from the heat and add the vanilla extract.

4 Beat the eggs, cream, and sweetener for 3–4 minutes (the mixture will remain fairly runny), then fold into the chocolate mixture. Pour into the pan and bake for 45 minutes, or until the top forms a crust.

5 Allow the cake to cool and then run a knife around the edges to loosen it from the pan.

6 Turn out the cake onto a serving plate and top with a mixture of blueberries and strawberries and serve with extra cream, if desired.

10 oz (300 g) bittersweet chocolate, 70 percent cocoa, broken into pieces

¾ cup (175 g) unsalted butter, cut into pieces

2 teaspoons vanilla extract

5 eggs, at room temperature

6 tablespoons whipping cream

4 teaspoons low-calorie granulated sweetener

To decorate

blueberries

strawberries

whipping cream

Nutritional values per serving

Carbs 20 g

Fat 19 g

Protein 8 g

Kcals 280

Peach Consommé with Raspberries

This really does have all the taste of summer—and it is full of immune-boosting nutrients too. If you want a more wintry version of the dish, serve it hot with a splash of brandy in the consommé.

Serves 4
Preparation time 10 minutes
Cooking time 20 minutes

1 Put the water, vanilla, star anise, cinnamon, and honey in a saucepan. Bring to a boil and simmer for 5 minutes.

2 Add all the peaches and poach for 5 minutes, then remove 4 of them with a slotted spoon and set aside to cool.

3 Add the lemon juice to the reserved liquid and simmer the remaining peaches for a further 10 minutes until mushy.

4 Meanwhile, gently peel the skins away from the cooled peaches and chill in the refrigerator.

5 Remove the pits from the mushy peaches and blend the pulp and cooking liquid in the blender. Push the puree through a muslin cloth and chill.

6 When ready to serve, place a poached peach in a serving bowl and pour one-quarter of the fruit consommé over the top. Decorate with raspberries and a sprig of mint and serve.

2½ cups (600 ml) water
1 vanilla pod
1 star anise
1 stick cinnamon
3 tablespoons honey
8 peaches
juice of 1 lemon

To decorate
1 cup (150 g) raspberries
mint sprigs

Nutritional values per serving
Carbs 29 g
Fat 0.3 g
Protein 3 g
Kcal 124

Pears in Dessert-wine Sauce

Using canned pears provides an extremely simple yet impressive twist on this classic dish. Pistachio nuts make a colorful change as a decoration, if you would like an alternative to the almonds.

Serves 4
Preparation time 1–2 minutes
Cooking time 15 minutes

1 cup (250 ml) orange juice

juice and zest of 1 unwaxed lemon

1 tablespoon brown sugar

1 cup (250 ml) dessert or sweet white wine

1 cinnamon stick

2–3 cloves

8 pears halves, canned in fruit juice, drained, and juice reserved

1 scant cup (75 g) toasted, flaked almonds

1 Put the orange juice, lemon juice and zest, sugar, wine, cinnamon stick, cloves, and reserved pear juice in a saucepan. Simmer over a medium heat for 15 minutes, or until reduced to one-quarter of its original volume.

2 Place the pears in the syrup and gently heat through.

3 Serve 2 pear halves per person, drizzled with the syrup and sprinkled with toasted almonds.

Nutritional values per serving

Carbs 27 g

Fat 10 g

Protein 4.8 g

Kcals 260

Bananas en Papillote

This is a really simple dessert that takes minutes to prepare and cook, and tastes indulgent if served with a generous dollop of crème fraîche or mascarpone. Carob is used as a natural chocolate substitute, although the flavors are quite different. You will find carob in health food stores.

Serves 4
Preparation time 2–3 minutes
Cooking time 3–4 minutes

1 Preheat the oven to 450°F.

2 Lightly grease 4 pieces of aluminum foil, each large enough to wrap a banana. Place a banana in the center and add a piece of cinnamon, 1 star anise, and a piece of vanilla pod.

3 Sprinkle with grated carob and one-quarter of the pineapple juice. Fold up to make an airtight pocket.

4 Place the sealed bananas on a baking pan and cook in the oven for 3–4 minutes. Alternatively cook on top of a barbecue or by the side of a bonfire—in both cases use double-thickness aluminum foil to prevent splits and spillages.

4 small, firm bananas
1 cinnamon stick, cut into 4
4 star anise
1 vanilla pod, cut into 4
2 tablespoons grated carob
⅓ cup (75 ml) pineapple juice

Nutritional values per serving
Carbs 30 g
Fat 0.5 g
Protein 1.7 g
Kcals 126

Red Fruit Salad

These fruits are good sources of lycopene and polyphenols, so they have great antioxidant properties. For a colorful garnish, finely chop some fresh basil—it works brilliantly with fruit.

Serves 4
Preparation time 5 minutes

1 Wash the strawberries, raspberries, and grapes and combine with the watermelon, vinegar, and port.

2 Chill in the refrigerator for 10–20 minutes. Serve with a little crème fraîche.

1¾ cups (250 g) fresh strawberries

1⅔ cups (250 g) fresh raspberries

2½ cups (250 g) seedless red grapes

1¾ cups (250 g) cubed watermelon

1 tablespoon balsamic vinegar

¼ cup (50 ml) port
crème fraîche, to serve

Nutritional values per serving

Carbs 21 g

Fat 0.3 g

Protein 1.9 g

Kcals 103

Mango and Lychee Mousse

This is a great pantry dessert—just make sure you buy the fruit canned in juice, not syrup. Mandarins are a good alternative to lychees, which can be a little sweet.

Serves 8
Preparation time 5 minutes

1 x 13-oz (400-g) can mango slices in juice

1 x 13-oz (400-g) can lychees

2 tablespoons low-fat plain yogurt

4 tablespoons ricotta

1 teaspoon fresh lime juice

1 tablespoon skim-milk powder

½ teaspoon vanilla extract

2 teaspoons clear honey

pared zest from unwaxed orange and lime, to decorate

1 Blend all the ingredients except the pared zest in a liquidizer or blender. If you want a thicker consistency, add 1 extra tablespoon of skim-milk powder.

2 Divide among 8 separate dessert glasses and chill for minimum of 30 minutes.

3 Decorate with a little pared orange and lime zest and serve.

Nutritional values per serving

Carbs 18 g

Fat 0.7 g

Protein 2.5 g

Kcals 84

Apple and Berry Strudel with Crème Anglaise

This recipe has all the appeal of an apple and berry pie without the high carb content. It is also incredibly quick to cook and can be popped in the oven while you are clearing away the dinner plates. The custard-style sauce uses eggs and arrowroot as a thickener instead of cornstarch, making it a great low-carb treat. It will last up to 3 days if kept in the refrigerator.

Serves 4
Preparation time 7 minutes
Cooking time 20 minutes

1 Preheat the oven to 300°F.

2 Put the grated apples, berries, cinnamon, and 1 teaspoon of the honey in a saucepan and sweat gently for about 5 minutes, or until the fruit is soft.

3 Brush the filo sheets with egg white and put 1 sheet on top of the other. Cut the sheets into quarters and place one-quarter of the fruit in the center of each rectangle. Tuck in the ends of the pastry and roll into a sausage shape.

4 Brush the rolls with the remaining honey and bake in the oven for 15 minutes, or until golden brown.

5 While the rolls are cooking, you can prepare the crème anglaise. Gently heat the milk and vanilla pod together for about 5 minutes. Bring to a boil and add the arrowroot paste, stirring until thickened. Cook gently for 2 minutes.

6 Place the sweetener and egg yolks in a mixing bowl and whisk until thick and pale. Whisk in the warm milk and, when thoroughly blended, transfer to a clean pan and reheat, stirring constantly. Do not allow to boil or it will curdle.

7 Remove the vanilla pod and pass the custard through a fine sieve. Mix in the mint and, when ready to serve, spoon over the strudel rolls. Garnish each roll with a sprig of mint.

2 cooking apples, grated

1 heaping cup (175 g) mixed berries

a pinch of cinnamon

1 tablespoon honey

2 sheets ready-made filo pastry

1 egg white

1 tablespoon mint, finely chopped

mint sprigs, to decorate

For the Crème Anglaise
(makes 2 cups [450 ml])

2 cups (450 ml) skim milk

1 vanilla pod

1 teaspoon arrowroot, mixed with a little water to make a paste

2 tablespoons low-calorie granulated sweetener

3 egg yolks

Nutritional values per serving

Carbs 32 g

Fat 9 g

Protein 9.5 g

Kcals 240

Passion Fruit Cream

This dish hails from Brazil and is absolutely delightful. The sweetness of the condensed milk is balanced by the sharpness of the passion fruit. For extra indulgence, scatter with curls of semisweet chocolate.

Serves 8
Preparation time 15 minutes

1 Break the passion fruits in half and empty the contents into a bowl. Stir briskly with a wooden spoon to loosen the pulp, then strain the juice through a sieve or a muslin cloth. Stir in the condensed milk and confectioner's sugar.

2 In another bowl, beat the cream until it forms stiff peaks. Fold one-third of the cream into the passion-fruit mixture, then gently fold in the rest of the cream until there are no streaks.

3 Put the dessert into a serving bowl and chill for a minimum of 30 minutes.

8 passion fruits

1⅔ cups (400 ml) sweetened condensed milk

1 tablespoon confectioner's sugar

2 cups (450 ml) whipping cream

Nutritional values per serving

Carbs 32 g

Fat 33 g

Protein 5.5 g

Kcals 440

Raspberry Tofu Crunch

This is as good for breakfast as it is for dessert. Vary the flavors by using strawberries or blackberries, and try a chopped pear instead of the apple.

Serves 3
Preparation time 5 minutes

12 oz (375 g) silken tofu

2 tablespoons honey

2 teaspoons vanilla extract

1 scant cup (125 g) raspberries

1 apple, cored and diced

½ cup (50 g) granola

2 tablespoons sliced almonds

1 Combine the tofu, honey, and vanilla in a blender and puree until smooth.

2 Transfer into a bowl and stir in the raspberries until the mixture is marbled with pink streaks.

3 Layer the tofu mixture into 3 serving glasses with the apple and granola. Top with the almonds, chill for 10–15 minutes, then serve.

Nutritional values per serving

Carbs 28 g

Fat 12 g

Protein 14 g

Kcals 276

Three Excellent Aïolis

The best way to spruce up a ready-made mayonnaise is to turn it into an unusual aïoli that can be used to enliven a plain salad, steamed vegetables, or pieces of fish or meat.

Red Chilli Aïoli

Makes ½ cup (125 ml)
Preparation time 1–2 minutes

Combine all the ingredients in a blender. Season and chill.

1 garlic clove, chopped

2 teaspoons mild chili powder

1 teaspoon paprika

4 tablespoons mayonnaise

2 tablespoons extra-virgin olive oil

¼ teaspoon ground cumin

a dash of lime juice

salt and pepper

Nutritional values per 1 tablespoon (15 ml)

Carbs 0 g

Fat 9 g

Protein 0 g

Kcals 86

Olive and Pesto Aïoli

Makes about ⅔ cup (175 ml)
Preparation time 1–2 minutes

Combine all the ingredients in a blender and process until smooth. Season and chill.

2 tablespoons green or red pesto

3 tablespoons mayonnaise

8–10 black olives

2 tablespoons olive oil

salt and pepper

Nutritional values per 1 tablespoon (15 ml)

Carbs 0.5 g

Fat 7 g

Protein 0.6 g

Kcals 66

Sesame and Ginger

Makes ¼ cup (65 ml)
Preparation time 1 minute

Stir the ingredients together, then chill.

3 tablespoons mayonnaise

4 teaspoons sesame oil

½ teaspoon ground ginger

Nutritional values per 1 tablespoon (15 ml)

Carbs 1 g

Fat 13 g

Protein 0 g

Kcals 121

Great Dressings

These three basic dressings are essential to great salads, but can also be drizzled over cooked vegetables for an interesting twist.

Balsamic

Makes about ¾ cup (200 ml)
Preparation time 10 minutes

Place all the ingredients in a pan over a low heat. Allow the flavors to infuse for 5 minutes, then strain and transfer to a glass bottle. Store in the refrigerator for up to 2 weeks.

⅓ cup (75 ml) balsamic vinegar

½ cup (125 ml) olive oil

½ teaspoon brown sugar

2 tablespoons chopped basil leaves

black pepper

Nutritional values per 5 teaspoons (25 ml)

Carbs 0.4 g

Fat 15 g

Protein 0 g

Kcals 144

Simple Vinaigrette

Makes about 1 cup (250 ml)
Preparation time 1–2 minutes

Whisk all the ingredients together and store in the refrigerator for up to 3 weeks. Stir before serving.

½ cup (125 ml) olive oil

½ cup (125 ml) white wine vinegar

2 tablespoons wholegrain mustard

salt and pepper

Nutritional values per 5 teaspoons (25 ml)

Carbs 0.2 g

Fat 15 g

Protein 0.3 g

Kcals 149

Thai dressing

Makes ½ cup plus 2 tablespoons (140 ml)
Preparation time 5 minutes

Combine all the ingredients in a bowl and store in the refrigerator for up to 1 week.

1 tablespoon sesame oil

⅓ cup (75 ml) light soy sauce

2 tablespoons lime juice

1 tablespoon brown sugar

2 red chilies, finely chopped

1 teaspoon fish sauce

Nutritional values per 5 teaspoons (25 ml)

Carbs 5 g

Fat 4 g

Protein 1 g

Kcals 58

Relishes and Salsas

Nothing beats a bit of something tasty on the side, and these quick recipes will jazz up anything from cold cuts to cheese.

Quick Hellish Relish

Many commercial sauces and relishes are full of sugar. This quick and very spicy relish is easy to make and gives a fiery kick to broiled meats and other sauces. It will keep for about a week in the fridge.

Serves 4–6
Preparation time 10 minutes

1 Preheat the broiler to hot. Line a rack with foil and on it place the onions, garlic, chilies, and the shrimp paste formed into a flat patty—if using anchovy paste, set it aside.
2 Quickly brown everything under the broiler on both sides. Allow the ingredients to cool.
3 Either chop all the broiled ingredients finely by hand or whiz in a blender. Chop the tomatoes finely and add to the blender along with the anchovy paste (if you are using), the fish sauce, and lime juice. Blend and check the seasoning.

6 shallots or small onions, left whole

3 garlic cloves, peeled

6 hot fresh chilies

½–1 teaspoon shrimp or anchovy paste (available from Asian stores)

6 cherry tomatoes

1 tablespoon fish sauce

1 tablespoon lime juice

salt (optional)

nutritional values per serving

Carbs 4.5 g

Fat 0 g

Protein 1.7 g

Kcals 24

Pineapple and Cucumber Salsa

Sweet pineapple is enlivened by fresh, crisp cucumber spiced up with garlic, chilies, and tangy lime juice. The heat of the chili is in the seeds and ribs, so remove them before mincing.

Serves 4
Preparation time 10 minutes, plus chilling time

1 Gently mix the diced pineapple, cucumber, and onion in a bowl.
2 Toss in the minced chili, garlic, lime zest, and lime juice. Cover and refrigerate for up to 2 hours before use.
3 Add basil and cilantro just before serving.

1⅓ cups (200 g) fresh, ripe diced pineapple

4-inch piece (150 g) seedless cucumber, peeled and diced

1 tablespoon diced red onion

1 teaspoon minced fresh red chili pepper

2 garlic cloves, finely chopped

½ teaspoon grated lime zest

2 tablespoons fresh lime juice

1 tablespoon finely slivered fresh basil

1 tablespoon coarsely chopped cilantro leaves

Nutritional values per 1 tablespoon (15 ml)

Carbs 6 g

Fat 0 g

Protein 0 g

Kcals 28

Savory Butters

Delicious if melted over vegetables or a steak, flavored butter can be kept in the fridge packed in small containers and covered with plastic wrap.

Herb Butter

Makes about ¾ cup (175 g)
Preparation time 5 minutes

Mix together all the ingredients, pack into small containers, and chill.

½ scant cup (100 g) unsalted butter, softened to room temperature

4 tablespoons mixed fresh herbs, finely chopped

2 tablespoon chives, chopped

a pinch of salt

black pepper (optional)

1 garlic clove, crushed (optional)

Nutritional value per 5 teaspoons (25 g)

Carbs 1 g

Fat 17 g

Protein 0.3 g

Kcals 155

Spicy Butter

Makes about ½ cup (125 g)
Preparation time 5 minutes

Combine all the ingredients, pack into small containers, and chill.

½ scant cup (100 g) unsalted butter

2 garlic cloves, finely chopped

1 teaspoon paprika

1 small red chili, seeded and finely chopped

¼ teaspoon ground cumin

a pinch of dried oregano

1 tablespoon olive oil

1 teaspoon chopped fresh cilantro

salt and pepper

Nutritional value per 5 teaspoons (25 g)

Carbs 0.5 g

Fat 22 g

Protein 0.3 g

Kcals 200

Index

fish
    fest 64–5
    organic 13
    poached in aromatic tamarind broth 63
    steamed fish with ginger and
        coconut milk 62
    see also individual fish
flourless chocolate cake 110–11
fruit
    density values 11
    GI levels 10
    and low-carb diets 12
    red fruit salad 116
    see also individual fruit

G

gado gado (Indonesian vegetables
    with peanut dressing) 91
gazpacho 22–3
ginger; steamed fish with ginger
    and coconut milk 62
globe artichokes
    mushroom and artichoke bake 99
    radicchio, artichoke, and walnut
        salad 34
glucose 9
Glycemic Index (GI) 9, 10
grapefruit; green olive and ruby
    grapefruit salad 42
grapes, chicken with red wine
    and 54–5
green beans
    gado gado 91
    green risotto 94–5
    with ham and garlic 102
green risotto 94–5

H

halibut in caper and white wine
    sauce 67
ham
    asparagus and prosciutto
        wraps 18–19
    green beans with ham and garlic 102
HDL (good) cholesterol 14
herb butter 125
hummus, Jerusalem artichoke 29
hydrogenated fat (trans fats) 14

I

Indonesian vegetables with peanut
    dressing (gado gado) 91
insulin resistance (Syndrome X) 8, 16

J

Jerusalem artichokes
    hummus 29
    radicchio, artichoke, and walnut
        salad 34

L

lamb
    bursa kebabs 77
    mustard lamb loin 80–1
LBM (lean body mass) 16
LDL (bad) cholesterol 14
lemon
    pan-roasted chicken with lemon
        and rosemary 57
    spinach, lentil, and lemon soup 24
    steamed asparagus with lemon and
        anchovy butter 108–9
    veal with wine and lemon 74–5
lemon grass
    chicken stir-fry with 52
    tamarind and lemon grass beef
        72–3
lentils
    duck breasts with lentils and
        mandarin marmalade 46–7
    spinach, lentil, and lemon soup 24
    warm puy lentil and goat cheese
        salad 36–7
lettuce, Romaine lettuce salad with
    Gorgonzola and walnuts 35
lime, okra with 104–5
lipids 13
liver; calves' liver and sage 76
lobsters; fish fest 64–5
low-carb diets 12–14, 16
lychees; mango and lychee mousse 117

M

mackerel; broiled fillet of mackerel
    with apple chutney 68–9
mango and lychee mousse 117
meat, organic 13
moderation 17
mushrooms
    mushroom and artichoke bake 99
    salmon baked with broccoli and
        morels 60–1
    shiitake mushroom omelette 28
mussels
    with chorizo 71
    fish fest 64–5
mustard lamb loin 80–1

O

obesity 7
okra with lime 104–5
olives
    braised quail with 56
    green olive and ruby grapefruit
        salad 42
    olive and pesto aïoli 122
omelettes
    onion frittata 21
    shiitake mushroom omelette 28
onions
    onion and fennel soup 25
    onion frittata 21
    quick tagine of red onions 100–1
oranges; duck breasts with lentils and
    mandarin marmalade 46–7
organic meat and fish 13
oyster sauce, Chinese greens in 103

P

passion fruit cream 120
pea, egg and tofu curry 98
peach consommé with raspberries 112
pears in dessert-wine sauce 113
pesto
    olive and pesto aïoli 122
    pan-fried chicken thighs with fresh
        pesto 50–1
phyto-nutrients 12
pine nuts, spinach with raisins and 106
pineapple and cucumber salsa 124
plums; duck breasts with baked
    Belgian endive 48
pork
    with Chinese cabbage 84–5
    marinated pork tenderloin 78–9
    rapid-fire ribs 82
protein 12–13
pumpkin and spinach puree 106

Q

quail; braised quail with olives 56
quick hellish relish 124
Quorn ground 97

R

radicchio, artichoke, and walnut
    salad 34
raisins; spinach with raisins and
    pine nuts 106
rapid-fire ribs 82

Acknowledgments

Executive Editor Nicky Hill
Editor Alice Tyler

Executive Art Editor Leigh Jones
Designer Anna Pow

Photography Gareth Sambidge
Styling Liz Hippisley

Home Economy Tonia George
Production Controller Aileen O'Reilly

Special thanks for loan of
cutlery, china, and glassware to:
David Mellor
(0044) 020 7730 4259
www.davidmellordesign.co.uk